More Power to Ya

THE PETRA DEVOTIONAL

by Bob Hartman

BIBLICAL INSIGHTS FROM TWO DECADES OF MUSICAL MINISTRY

More Power to Ya

THE PETRA DEVOTIONAL

More Power to Ya

THE PETRA DEVOTIONAL

by Bob Hartman

BIBLICAL INSIGHTS FROM TWO DECADES
OF MUSICAL MINISTRY

Standard Publishing
Cincinnati, Ohio

Scripture quotations are taken from the HOLY BIBLE, NEW INTERNA-
TIONAL VERSION®. NIV®. Copyright © 1973, 1978, 1984 by International
Bible Society. Used by permission of Zondervan Publishing House. All rights
reserved. Used by permission.

Edited by Dale Reeves
Cover illustration by Jeff Haynie
Cover and inside design by Franke Design Company
Additional interior design by Dina Sorn
Special thanks to Sherry Singletary for sharing her Petra memorabilia

Library of Congress Cataloging-in-Publication Data:
Available upon request

The Standard Publishing Company, Cincinnati, Ohio
A Division of Standex International Corporation

04   03   02   01   00   99   98   97   5   4   3   2   1

DEDICATION

I dedicate this book to my beautiful wife, Kim, who has
faithfully stood by my side and served the ministry of Petra for
17 years, and to my son, Jeffrey, who I hope will follow in
my footsteps as I attempt to follow our Savior.

Bob Hartman is available for speaking engagements through
Mike Atkins management at (615) 298-2211.

Check out Petra's web page. The address is:
http://www.Wordrecords.com/Petra/

TABLE OF CONTENTS

FOREWORD

I have felt the desire to write this book for quite some time, and my decision to stop touring with the band allowed me the time. Over the many years of Petra's ministry, we have received countless letters from people, telling us how our song lyrics have made such a positive impact in their spiritual lives. We have always placed a great emphasis on making our lyrics biblically sound. We have even received letters from pastors who have used our lyrics as illustrations for their sermons. No greater compliment could be paid to us, and I want to give all the praise and glory to our Lord and God.

During the writing of this book, I was reminded over and over again of God's goodness toward us in allowing us to serve Him for so many years. I pray that the message of this book comes through loud and clear: You don't have to be in a band or speak from a pulpit to serve God! We serve Him every day of our lives when we faithfully follow Him. I hope these writings will bring back fond memories for you as they did for me. But most of all, I hope you are challenged to walk more closely with Jesus, serving Him with passion as the power of God's Word works in your life. More Power to Ya!

Bob Hartman

PETRASPECTIVE 1974–1979

Petra (1974)

Song List

Walkin' in the Light
Mountains and Valleys
Lucas McGraw
Backslidin' Blues
I'm Not Ashamed
Wake Up
Get Back to the Bible
Gonna Fly Away
Storm Comin'
Parting Thought

This album was recorded in late 1973 on a shoestring budget in a 16-track studio in South Pekin, Illinois. We were new Christians who had never been in a studio before and we were very green. The music reflected the dual guitar style of the band with many double leads. The lyrics reflected the newness, innocence and sincerity of our faith.

The album also contains a novelty song that, to this day, is one of the most requested songs in Petra's history—"Lucas McGraw." In our concerts, we were doing a lighthearted bluegrass set of which "Lucas McGraw" was the centerpiece. At our concerts in cities around the world, it is not unusual to see a banner that reads "Lucas McGraw."

Come and Join Us (1977)

Song List

God Gave Rock and Roll to You

Ask Him In

Sally

Without You I Would Surely Die

Come and Join Us

Where Can I Go

Holy Ghost Power

Woman Don't You Know

God Gave Rock and Roll to You (Reprise)

Our second album was recorded at the same studio in Illinois as our first, only on 24 tracks. We wanted to call the record *God Gave Rock and Roll to You*, but the record company had better insight into the conservative nature of many of the Christian bookstores where the record would be sold. Also, by the record company's choice, the song "Killing My Old Man" was dropped, much to our disappointment. The song was re-recorded for the *Never Say Die* record several years later.

The lyrics were more pre-evangelistic than the first record, in keeping with the predominantly evangelistic mission of the band at the time. Greg X. Volz made his first guest appearance with Petra on this album.

Washes Whiter Than (1979)

Song List

I'm Thankful

Why Should the Father Bother?

Morning Star

Magic Mirror

Mary's Song

Yahweh Love

(Couldn't Find Love) Without You

Taste and See

Magic Words

Deep Love

Recorded in Florida, this record represented a stylistic departure for the band with the absence of dual guitars and the addition of keyboards. Overall, *Washes Whiter Than* was intentionally less aggressive, as Petra hoped to move more into the mainstream of Christian music. This turned out to be a mistake in many ways. We failed to win a new audience and alienated many of our fans.

"Why Should The Father Bother?" was the "silver lining," however, reaching number three on the Christian radio charts—Petra's first Christian radio success. Again, Greg X. Volz made a guest appearance. He began touring with the band after the release of this record.

WALKIN' IN THE LIGHT

"But if we walk in the light, as he is in the light, we have fellowship with one another, and the blood of Jesus, his Son, purifies us from all sin."
1 John 1:7

Walkin' in the Light

Words and music by Bob Hartman
© 1974 by Petsong Publishing/SESAC.
All rights reserved. Used by permission.

I'm rockin' with the Rock,
rollin' on the road that
takes me to the King.
I've been up and down your city,
and I wish you could see all
the love you need.

Chorus
Walkin' in the light every day and night,
livin' in the Spirit is really out of sight.
Walkin' in the light every day and night,
livin' in the Spirit is really out of sight.

I know you've given me Your Spirit,
peace in my heart, a new song to sing.
I'm giving love to all of my brothers
and I wish you could see all
the joy it brings.

Walkin' in the light every day and night,
livin' in the Spirit is really out of sight.
Walkin' in the light every day and night,
livin' in the Spirit is really out of sight.

I'm rockin' with the Rock,
rollin' on the road that
takes me to the King.
I'm tellin' all my friends about You
and I wish they could see
all the love You bring.

I am a little embarrassed when I read the lyrics I wrote in the earliest Petra songs. I knew so little of God's Word, but I was eager to share in song what I *had* learned. "Walkin' in the Light" attempted to share the excitement I felt when I realized what it was like to walk with God.

In 1 John 1, a contrast is made—the contrast of light and darkness. Darkness is where we once were, and the light is where God is because He is light. It is possible for a Christian to still walk in darkness (v. 6). Our "walk" is our conduct. If our conduct is in darkness—sin—then we can't have fellowship with God because there is no darkness in Him. Fellowship means "to have in common with." Fellowship with God is, therefore, to have our conduct in common with His holiness. Obviously, this is not to be taken that we will never sin, for we sin in word, thought and deed every day. But when we hate the things He hates and love the things He loves, His blood continually cleanses us from sin.

I have to frequently ask myself if I love the things He loves and hate the things He hates. Am I enamored by sin, or does it turn my stomach as it does God's? The more we walk in the light and have fellowship with Him, the easier it is to recognize darkness. It is like walking from bright sunlight into a darkened room. At first, the contrast is startling and we can't see a thing, but the longer we stay out of the light, the more our eyes adjust and things start to appear as "normal" in the darkness.

May God help you and me today to keep on walking in the light and never lose sight of that contrast.

LUCAS MCGRAW

"In everything set them an example by doing what is good." Titus 2:7

Lucas McGraw

Lucas McGraw, what's come over you?
We're beginnin' to think you're
touched. We hear ya got religion,
ya ain't been 'round to see us much.
Ya threw away your corncob pipe
and your jug of moonshine brew.
And we hear you ain't been doin'
all those things you used to do.

Lucas McGraw, what's come over you?
You're shavin' ev'ry day.
You ain't been chasin' women
and you kissed your wife today.
You went to church last Sunday
and ya shook the preacher's hand.
And they say you been talkin'
'bout a home beyond this land.

Lucas McGraw, what's come over you?
Ya never cuss no more.
We hear you ain't been feudin',
you hung your rifle by the door.
Ya take a bath each Sunday
if ya need it or not.
And ya go to work on Monday
Even when it's hot.

Lucas McGraw, what's come over you?
We're beginnin' to think you're
touched. We hear ya got religion,
ya ain't been 'round to see us much.
But ya know we've all been wonderin'
if what ya got just might be real.
and all the while we're laughin',
is it really God, is it really God,
is it really God you feel?

For some reason unknown to me, this novelty song on our first album has maintained a cultlike popularity throughout our history—even in foreign countries! We have seen banners from one end of our travels to the other bearing the infamous name from this narrative of a converted hillbilly, as told by his friends. In some of our earliest concerts, we performed a comedy bluegrass set as an icebreaker, climaxing with "Lucas McGraw." The message behind the humor is this: as his old friends began to see his life change, they started to consider the reality of God.

I remember being surprised at the response of my old friends to my new-found faith. I expected them to listen and believe. Most of them did neither at first! It wasn't until they saw some dramatic changes in my life that I began to sense their respect. They knew that a faith that doesn't change the way you live is a faith not worth having. As they began to see my consistency and perseverance, they grew more curious and I was able to share God's love with them. I moved away and no longer see them, but I have been told that some believe today because they saw what happened to me.

If you want your friends to see the truth, they must be allowed to see Christ in you. We will never know till Heaven what has grown from the seeds of our testimony sown through our good works.

WHY SHOULD THE FATHER BOTHER?

"For you did not receive a spirit that makes you a slave again to fear, but you received the Spirit of sonship. And by him we city, ' Abba, Father.'"
Romans 8:15

Why Should the Father Bother?

Chorus
Why should the Father bother
to call us His children?
Why should the Spirit
hear it when we pray?
Why should the Father bother
to be concerned with all our needs?
It's all because of what the Son has done.

Once we were lost out on the ocean
with no direction or devotion,
tossed about by every wind and wave.
Now we are in the world, not of it, and
we can surely rise above it, because the
Lord has risen from the grave.

Repeat chorus

And we cry, "Abba, Father,"
"Abba, Father," "Abba, Father"
"Abba, Father," "Abba, Father,"
"Abba, Father."

Once we were strangers from the
promise, we were doubters worse
than Thomas—until the Spirit
opened up our eyes.
Now He has offered us adoption
and we have taken up the option
to be his family eternally.

Repeat chorus

People always told me that becoming a parent changes your life. I had no idea of the magnitude of that change until my wife and I adopted our son. I consider it one of the greatest moments of my life when his beautiful blue eyes looked up into mine and he called me "Daddy."

Our relationship has brought new understanding to this passage in Romans, as well as new meaning to an old song from *Washes Whiter Than*. It is no surprise that Paul wrote of spiritual adoption to the Romans. Jewish law did not allow for adoption, but Roman law did. The word *adoption*, here, literally means "to be brought forward as a legitimate son with all the rights and privileges of a natural son."

As Christians, we are all adopted as children of God, but just as in Roman law, there are obstacles to overcome: namely, we are naturally born outside of God's family, and we are lawbreakers. To take care of the first problem, we are born again into God's family, but the second problem demands that a penalty be paid. The Judge Himself stepped down from His throne and paid the penalty for us! Now we are His legal children and joint-heirs to all He has! The word *power*, in John 1: 12 (RSV), actually means the "legal right" to be called His children. Why should the Father bother to call us His children? It's all because of what the Son has done!

As His spiritual children, we have every right to call Him "Daddy," which is what "Abba" means in Aramaic. Take some time today to talk with Him.

PETRASPECTIVE 1980-1983

Never Say Die (1981)

Song List

The Coloring Song
Chameleon
Angel of Light
Killing My Old Man
Without Him We Can Do Nothing
Never Say Die
I Can Be Friends With You
For Annie
Father of Lights
Praise Ye the Lord

This record marked the first recording with Greg X. Volz as a permanent member of the band. It was a return to the "no holds barred" aggressive style of the first two recordings that would characterize the band throughout the '80s. *Never Say Die* enjoyed the most Christian airplay in Petra's history.

"The Coloring Song" topped every Christian radio chart simultaneously. "For Annie," a song about teen suicide, touched many lives positively, for which I am eternally grateful.

More Power to Ya (1982)

Song List

Stand Up

Second Wind

More Power to Ya

Judas' Kiss

Rose Colored Stained Glass Windows

Run for the Prize

All Over Me

Let Everything That Hath Breath

Road to Zion

Disciple

Perhaps my favorite album, *More Power to Ya* was recorded in the desert in West Texas, which may have contributed to what I call the "vibe" of the record. Again, we were successful at radio with the title cut, as well as "Road to Zion," but the recording also contained several rock songs that became concert favorites, such as "Judas' Kiss" and "Let Everything That Hath Breath." This record helped Petra find its audience and its ministry.

Not of This World (1983)

Song List

Visions (Doxology)
Not of This World
Bema Seat
Grave Robber
Blinded Eyes
Not by Sight
Lift Him Up
Pied Piper
Occupy
Godpleaser
Visions (Reprise)

I consider this to be the musical equivalent of a "sequel" to the previous recording. We again scored at Christian radio with the title song and "Grave Robber," and added concert favorites such as "Godpleaser," "Not by Sight," "Bema Seat" and "Lift Him Up." The tour that followed this record remains a very fond memory for me personally.

THE COLORING SONG

"' Come now, let us reason together,' says the LORD.
' Though your sins are like scarlet, they shall be as
white as snow; though they are red as crimson, they
shall be like wool.'"
Isaiah 1:18

The Coloring Song

Red is the color of the blood that flowed
down the face of someone who loved us
so. He's the perfect man, He's the
Lord's own Son. He's the Lamb of God,
He's the only one that can give us life,
that can make us grow, that can
make the love between us flow.

Blue is the color of a heart so cold that
will not bend when the story's told of
the love of God for a sinful race, of the
blood that flowed down Jesus' face,
that can give us life, that can make us
grow, that can keep our hearts
from growing cold.

Gold is the color of the morning sun
that shines so freely on everyone.
It's the sun above that keeps us warm;
it's the Son of love that calms the storm,
that can give us life, that can make us
grow, that can turn our
mornings into gold.

Brown is the color of the autumn leaves
when the winter comes to the barren
trees. There is birth; there is death;
there is a plan, and there's just one God,
and there's just one Man that can give us
life, that can make us grow, that can
make our sins as white as snow;
that can give us life, that can make us
grow, that can turn our mornings into
gold; that can give us life, that can make
us grow, that can keep our hearts from
growing cold; that can give us life, that
can make us grow, that can
make the love between us flow.

This song was written by David Eden,
who was part of an early Christian rock
band called "E Band," of which Greg X.
Volz was also a member. As we were
looking for songs for our *Never Say
Die* album, this never-before-recorded
song came up. It represented a straight-
forward, childlike faith that was charac-
teristic of the Jesus Movement of the
early '70s. This was a very special time
for me, for it is when I found Christ.

The Jesus Movement, for those too
young to remember, was a very special
move of the Holy Spirit which brought
thousands of people, mostly hippies
fresh from the counterculture of the late
'60s, to a vibrant saving faith in Jesus
Christ. Many things about that period

are still fresh in my memory, still a source of blessing and encouragement. It was a genuine Holy Spirit revival, and I feel privileged to have witnessed it. People came to the Lord on the street, in coffeehouses, on the beach, in churches and anywhere else there was a faithful convert to share his faith. There were concerts where the better part of the audience was on their knees weeping before the Lord. Altar calls would leave scarcely a soul in the audience.

Many times since, I have tried to figure out the "magic formula" of that time and I have come to the conclusion that it was simply a move of God. We knew a lot less back then. We thought that it was supposed to work that way. People prayed and spoke out in faith, and God moved. Perhaps we knew more than we realized.

God meant for our faith to be simple. It is a faith for everyone. I hope that you will not be moved from the simplicity of the gospel, for in that simplicity lies the power of God unto salvation.

CHAMELEON

"For you were once darkness, but now you are light in the Lord. Live as children of light."
Ephesians 5:8

Chameleon

Words and music by Bob Hartman
© 1981 Dawn Treader Music/SESAC (a division of Star Song). All rights reserved. International copyright secured. Used by permission.

You want the best of both worlds, but you're not getting either. You seem content to ride the fence when you know which side is greener. Some run hot and some run cold and some run from their Maker. Some run the risk of losing all with lukewarm friends and fakers.

Chorus
Chameleon, you blend with your surroundings. Chameleon, no one knows where you come from. Chameleon, you change with every situation, compromising dedication.

You compromise each word you say so inoffensively. You only want to hide behind your anonymity. You struggle for acceptance and it takes you to extremes. The smile you hide your face behind is not all that it seems.

Come out, come out, come out from among them; come out, come out, come out and be free.

There is no gray, no neutral ground; there's only black and white, and nothing in between the two to turn a wrong into right. There is no time for your charade, you've got to make your stand. When salt has lost its savor, the world becomes so bland.

Repeat chorus

A chameleon is a curious reptile with a rather unique defense system. It has the ability to change the color of its skin according to its surroundings. It is able to blend in instead of sticking out. This song was written about chameleon Christians, those who "blend in" with whatever crowd they happen to be with at the time. They fall right in with the behavior patterns or attitudes of whomever they are with.

We are afraid our friends won't like us or that they will feel we are "holier than thou" if we tell them we are bothered by what is happening around us. All of us want to have friends and be popular, but we must weigh the cost of popularity with the cost of compromising our testimony. Once we compromise our testimony, we will never be able to share Christ with them without it coming back to haunt us. Our testimony is the most powerful soul-winning weapon in our arsenal, and I believe Satan wants nothing more than to destroy it. We overcome by the blood of the Lamb and the word of our testimony (Revelation 12:11), and we do so by living as children of light in a world of darkness.

A little light goes a long way. Where I live, we have frequent power outages so we keep candles close at hand. When a room is pitch black, one candle makes the difference between people stumbling or finding their way. We are called to share the light.

Try identifying with Christ in some small way when you first meet someone. You will know right away if they want to be your friend. You will be put in fewer compromising situations, you will have stayed true to your convictions, and most of all, you will not be a "chameleon."

FOR ANNIE

"' If a man owns a hundred sheep, and one of them wanders away, will he not leave the ninety-nine on the hills and go to look for the one that wandered off? And if he finds it, I tell you the truth, he is happier about that one sheep than about the ninety-nine . . . . In the same way your Father in heaven is not willing that any of these little ones should be lost.'" Matthew 18:12-14

For Annie

No one ever noticed Annie weeping, people all around, but she was all alone. Mama's got her meetings and Daddy's got his job, but no one's got the time, so Annie's on her own. No one ever knew her desperation, people couldn't hear her cry out silently. Locked inside the bathroom she grabs a jar of pills; the medicine that cures becomes the poison that kills.

Chorus

And it's too late for Annie, she's gone away for good. There's so much we could tell her and now we wish we could, but it's too late, it's too late for Annie.

Sadness fills the hearts of Annie's family, Daddy tries to comfort Mama uselessly. They hoped she knew they loved her, but they really didn't know. They just want to know why did their baby go?

Repeat chorus

If only we'd have known her situation, we'd have tried to stop this useless tragedy. Annie's lost forever, never to be found, but there are lots of others like her all around. And it's not too late for Annie, she could be next to you. Don't miss the chance to tell her before her life is through. We gotta tell her Jesus loves her, tell her Jesus cares, tell her He can free her and her burdens bear. It's not too late.

After watching a television special about the alarming increase in teenage suicide, I was moved to write this song, which was then recorded on *Never Say Die*. Annie, although not a real person, could represent someone you know. We have probably gotten more response to this song than any other we have ever recorded. Perhaps it strikes a nerve in teenagers who can relate to how she felt. Many young people have come up to me over the years to tell me that, because of this song, they decided not to take their own life. Nothing could be more gratifying than knowing we reached someone with the hope we have in Christ.

Matthew **18:12-14** emphasizes the importance of each individual in the sight of God. Even though the shepherd still had ninety-nine sheep left, the one which was lost was important enough to go after. People as disturbed as Annie usually don't come to us. We have to pursue *them* at the risk of intruding into their personal lives in a way in which they are not comfortable. Just like pursuing a lost sheep, it can be risky. But if our efforts can convince them that their life is important to us and even more important to God, they just might have enough courage to face another day.

We never know when a person is close to taking his own life. We just have to reach out to anybody who seems to be troubled and tell her that Jesus loves her and cares about her. So look for Annie today. She could be right next to you.

MORE POWER TO YA

"But those who hope in the LORD will renew their strength. They will soar on wings like eagles; they will run and not grow weary, they will walk and not be faint."   Isaiah 40:31

More Power to Ya

Words and music by Bob Hartman
© 1982 Dawn Treader Music/SESAC
(a division of Star Song). All rights reserved.
International copyright secured. Used by permission.

You say you've been feeling weaker,
weaker by the day, you say you can't
make the joy of your salvation stay.
But good things come to them that wait,
not to those who hesitate, so hurry up
and wait upon the Lord.

Chorus
More power to ya when you're standing
on His word, when you're trusting
with your whole heart in
the message you have heard.
More power to ya when we're all
in one accord. They that wait
upon the Lord, they shall renew,
they shall renew their strength.

Jesus promised His disciples
He'd give strength to them.
Jesus told them all to tarry in Jerusalem.
When they were all in one accord the
power of His Spirit poured, and they
began to turn the world around.

Repeat chorus

So be strong in the Lord and in the
power of His might, put on all His
armor and fight the good fight.
In all of our weakness He becomes so
strong, and He gives us the power
and the strength to carry on.

The recording of *More Power to Ya* in a studio in the West Texas desert is one of my most memorable experiences with Petra. There was something very special about the isolation of the desert that, I believe, brought out the unique "vibe" of that recording. The vastness of the desert sky at night and the endless variety of wildlife are etched in my memory forever.

This title song was very much a part of that vibe. It is a song about spiritual power and strength. Every Christian goes through times of strength and times of weakness. Often our greatest times of weakness follow immediately after our greatest times of strength. We sometimes seem to go from the highest mountain to the lowest valley. God uses our times of weakness to show us that our strength comes from Him and not ourselves. God used this fact to humble me many times during my ministry with Petra.

We need to know how to plug in and get recharged! The *King James Version* calls this time of recharging "waiting" upon the Lord. If we want to renew our strength, we must spend time with Him and allow Him to minister to us through His Word. Even Jesus Himself needed these times. There are many times in the Gospels when Jesus went off by Himself to pray after exhausting Himself in ministry. The sooner we learn and practice this principle, the sooner we will feel His strength again.

The next time you feel as if God has used you, get ready! Prepare for a time of testing and weakness by getting alone with God immediately. Hurry up and wait upon the Lord!

1980 **8** 1983

JUDAS' KISS

"While he was still speaking a crowd came up, and the man who was called Judas, one of the Twelve, was leading them. He approached Jesus to kiss him, but Jesus asked him, 'Judas, are you betraying the Son of Man with a kiss?'"
Luke **22:47, 48**

Judas' Kiss

I wonder how it makes You feel when
the prodigal won't come home.
I wonder how it makes You feel when
he'd rather be on his own.
I wonder what it's like for You
when a lamb has gone astray.
I wonder what it's like for You
when Your children disobey.

Chorus
It must be like another thorn
stuck in Your brow.
It must be like another
close friend's broken vow.
It must be like another nail
right through Your wrist.
It must be just like,
just like Judas' kiss.

I wonder how it makes You feel
when no one seeks Your face.
I wonder how it makes You feel
when they give up in the race.
I wonder what it's like for You
when they willingly disobey.
I wonder what it's like for You
when they willingly walk away.

It must be like another thorn
stuck in Your brow.
It must be like another
close friend's broken vow.
It must be like another nail
right through Your wrist.
It must be just like,
just like Judas' kiss.

I wrote "Judas' Kiss" while visiting my mother, who was in the hospital for surgery for a very serious cancer which took her life just a few years later. During that time, I took the opportunity to reflect on many things. Times like that make a person really consider the meaning of life. I started thinking about how Jesus must have felt when He was betrayed. How does He feel now when someone turns away from Him? How does He feel when a prodigal son won't return home, but instead continues in his own way? And, in particular, how did He feel when He was betrayed by one of His own disciples, Judas?

Much has been said about the physical

pain that Jesus suffered when He was taken and beaten, whipped, spat upon and eventually nailed to a cross to die. But I think we underestimate the emotional and spiritual pain He suffered.

What was it like for the perfect, sinless Son of God to feel the weight of the sins of the world? There can be no human empathy for this in the minds of fallen men. How did it feel for the Author of love itself to be betrayed by, of all things, a kiss? In this Scripture, He seems to be saying, "Judas, you knew me, you walked with me, you saw me heal and deliver, you saw my love for you as well as the others, and now, you would betray me with the very sign of love between two people—a kiss?" I think His heart was breaking as He spoke these words.

I imagine we, who call ourselves His followers, can also break His heart. And yet, He still loves us in an immeasurable way. It is that kind of love that causes the prodigal to find his way home, and the errant servant to return to his Master, and you and me to fall before His throne of grace to beg for mercy.

ROAD TO ZION

"Blessed are those whose strength is in you, who have set their hearts on pilgrimage. As they pass through the Valley of Baca, they make it a place of springs; the autumn rains also cover it with pools. They go from strength to strength, till each appears before God in Zion."   Psalm 84:5-7

Road to Zion

Words and music by Mike Hudson
© 1982 Shepherd's Fold Music/BMI (a division of Star Song). All rights reserved. International copyright secured. Used by permission.

There is a way that leads to life,
the few that find it never die,
past mountain peaks graced white with
snow the way grows brighter as it goes.

Chorus
There is a road inside of you,
inside of me there is one too.
No stumbling pilgrim in the dark,
the road to Zion's in your heart,
the road to Zion's in your heart.

The river runs beside the road,
its waters living as they flow.
In liquid voice the water calls,
on thirsty knees a pilgrim falls.

Repeat chorus

Sometimes a shadow dark and cold
lays like a mist across the road.
But be encouraged by the sight,
where there's a shadow there's a light.

Sometimes it's good to look back
down—we've come so far,
we've gained such ground.
But joy is not in where we've been,
joy is who's waiting at the end.

Repeat chorus

"Road to Zion," written by Mike Hudson, describes the believers' pilgrim journey. Zion is the city of God—Heaven. As David wrote this psalm, he may have had the journey to Jerusalem in mind. There are many parallels for us in our journey. The way to Jerusalem was hard and long and filled with many dangers. A person had to "set his heart" before leaving. So must we set our hearts on the things above in order to survive the journey.

The Valley of Baca can also mean "the valley of weeping." There will be many bright and sunny spots, quiet resting places and pleasant memories along the way, but at some time, we must go through the valley of weeping. The true pilgrim passes through the valley of weeping and makes it a place of refreshment. We may face many bitter experiences on our journey, but they become hidden well-springs of refreshment as we learn and grow. They are as much a part of the journey as the warm sunny meadows. They help us to go from "strength to strength."

I can remember riding my bicycle home from school as a young man in Ohio. The last part of the journey was uphill and the ice-cold westerly wind blew in my face and chilled me to the bone. There were many times I thought about giving up, but I knew as I reached the top of the hill and turned the corner, my warm house was waiting and my journey was over.

Each day we live is one day closer to Zion. Along the road, there are many joys and victories, heartaches and trials, but when we finally arrive and enter into rest, it will all be worth it. Be of good cheer, pilgrim, that road to Zion is in your heart.

NOT OF THIS WORLD

"Jesus said, 'My kingdom is not of this world.'"
John 18:36

Not of This World

We are pilgrims in a strange land, we
are so far from our homeland.
With each passing day it seems so clear
this world will never want us here.
We're not welcome in this world of
wrong, we are foreigners
who don't belong.

Chorus
We are strangers, we are aliens,
we are not of this world.

We are envoys, we must tarry,
with this message we must carry.
There's so much to do before we leave,
with so many more who may believe.
Our mission here can never fail,
and the gates of Hell will not prevail.

We are strangers, we are aliens,
we are not of this world.

Jesus told us men would hate us
but we must be of good cheer.
He has overcome this world
of darkness and soon we will
depart from here.

To be a Christian is to belong to an unseen kingdom. We undergo a change of citizenship when we accept Christ as our Lord, "for he has rescued us from the dominion of darkness and brought us into the kingdom of the Son he loves" (Colossians 1:13). We have become citizens of Heaven and, therefore, strangers and pilgrims in this world.

Petra has toured in Europe many times over the years, and in so doing, we have gotten a glimpse of what it means to be strangers and aliens. Although we have always been warmly received by our audiences, Americans are not the most loved people in some countries. We are often thought of as being demanding, loud, rude and thinking that the world revolves around the United

States. At times, there were band members who did their part to perpetuate this notion! But we endured the small inconveniences of tiny hotel rooms with no air conditioning and beds the size of a postage stamp for a reason: We were called to bring the good news of the gospel to all the world.

Jesus told us that as citizens of Heaven we would endure more than just a few inconveniences. The world would hate us, imprison us and possibly kill us because of Him. To Christians in some parts of the world, persecution is a present reality. But Jesus followed these warnings with one of the most encouraging verses in the Bible, a verse we should hide in our hearts and bring to remembrance every day: "'I have told you these things, so that in me you may have peace. In this world you will have trouble. But take heart! I have overcome the world'" (John 16:33).

We must daily remind ourselves that we are no longer part of this world system, but rather missionaries from our true homeland in Heaven.

BEMA SEAT

"For we must all appear before the judgment seat of Christ, that each one may receive what is due him for the things done while in the body, whether good or bad."   *2 Corinthians 5:10*

Bema Seat

When our labor all retire there
will be a trial by fire.
Will your treasure pass the test
or will it burn up with the rest?
You may build upon a sure foundation
with your building in dilapidation.
When it all comes down to rubble
will it be wood, hay and stubble,
Or precious stones, gold and silver—
are you really sure?

Chorus
And we all will stand at the Bema Seat,
all will be revealed—it will be complete.
Will there be reward in the fiery heat,
when we see our lives at the Bema Seat?

Every talent will be surely counted,
every word will have to be accounted.
Not a story will be left untold, we will
stand and watch the truth unfold.
Every score will be evened;
nothing to defend.

Every building will be shaken,
every motive will be tried.
He'll give reward to the faithful,
will you receive or be denied?

Repeat chorus

There is good news and bad news in this verse! The bad news is that we as Christians will all be judged for our works. The good news is that it will be our Savior who judges us! The Greek word *bema* is translated "judgment seat" in this verse. It was the place of judgment in the Greek and Roman courts, a place familiar to Paul. This is a judgment of our works, not our souls! It is our loving Redeemer who will be the Judge.

1 Corinthians 3:12-15 goes into more detail on the subject: "If any man builds on this foundation using gold, silver, costly stones, wood, hay or straw, his work will be shown for what it is, because the Day will bring it to light. It

will be revealed with fire, and the fire will test the quality of each man's work. If what he has built survives, he will receive his reward. If it is burned up, he will suffer loss; he himself will be saved, but only as one escaping through the flames."

There will surely be many surprises that day! Everything will be brought to light and judged by fire. Many things we thought would be rewarded will be consumed by fire. Many behind-the-scenes servants will be given the greatest rewards. Consider it Heaven's "quality control." Hopefully we are all building on the same foundation which is Jesus Christ, but we are using a variety of building materials. Only the best "materials" will survive this fire.

We should inspect our buildings periodically to assess how they look. Are we up to code? Are we spending our lives in the right way? Better to be honest with ourselves now than to barely escape through the flames of His consuming fire at the Bema seat!

12

GODPLEASER

" And when you pray, do not be like the hypocrites, for they love to pray standing in the synagogues and on the street corners to be seen by men. I tell you the truth, they have received their reward in full.'"

Matthew 6:5

Godpleaser

Words and Music by Bob Hartman
© 1983 Dawn Treader Music/SESAC (a division of Star Song). All rights reserved. International copyright secured. Used by permission.

So many voices telling me which way to go, so many choices come from those think they know. There's a way that seems right to a man but it only brings him death. I wanna go the way that leads to life till I draw my dying breath.

Chorus
Don't wanna be a manpleaser—I wanna be a Godpleaser, I just want to have the wisdom to discern the two apart. Don't wanna be a manpleaser—I wanna be a Godpleaser, I just want to do the things that please the Father's heart.

Some make a sacrifice and never let it show, some make a point of letting everybody know. Some will live their lives as unto men and they have their reward. I just wanna do everything I do with all my heart unto the Lord.

Repeat chorus

I just want my life to glorify His Son to make my Father proud that I'm His child before I'm done, no need to pat me on the back or stop to shake my hand. I just want to hear my Father say, "Well done," "Well done," I just want to hear my Father say, "Well done."

Repeat chorus

Spiritual pride is one of the most difficult things to spot in our own lives and in the lives of others because it is always wrapped up in a robe of piety that, in outward appearance, can look very sincere. The essence of spiritual pride is brought out in this verse from Matthew.

The hypocrites prayed standing in the synagogues and on the street corners with the motive of being seen by men. It was their *motive* that qualified them as hypocrites. Their goal was to be thought of highly by men. They were "menpleasers." To be a "Godpleaser" is to have a different motive. A Godpleaser may do many of the same things, but in his heart of hearts, he cares only about one thing: pleasing God.

It takes the help of the Holy Spirit and very objective self-examination for us to see our own motives. It also takes a firm conviction of where we want our reward to be. Jesus said that these hypocrites already had their reward in full. Their reward was being seen by men. Do we want our reward to be on this earth or in the kingdom of Heaven?

Many times I have asked myself this question before walking on a stage. Is my only reward a standing ovation? I sincerely hope not. Petra always prays that what we do on stage will be pleasing to God.

God alone can righteously judge all of our motives, and He will. I only hope that when I finally see Him face to face, I am welcomed with "Well done, good and faithful servant, here is your reward." Decide to be a Godpleaser today!

PETRA

**CAPTURED
IN TIME & SPACE**

Beat the System (1984)

Song List

Beat the System
Computer Brains
Clean
It Is Finished
Voice in the Wind
God Gave Rock and Roll to You
Witch Hunt
Hollow Eyes
Speak to the Sky
Adonai

Another departure stylistically, *Beat the System* reflects the "techno" sounds that were current at the time. Although we had little success at radio with "Hollow Eyes," the song made a statement about world hunger that I believe is relevant for all times. Songs such as the title cut, "Clean" and "Adonai" ushered in a new professionalism to our concerts. The tour touched many lives, evidenced by the number of testimonies that continue to surface.

Captured in Time and Space (1985)

Song List

Beat the System
Computer Brains
Clean
Grave Robber
Speak to the Sky
Hollow Eyes
Rock Medley: *Stand Up/
Not by Sight/Judas' Kiss*
Mellow Medley: *Coloring
Song/Road to Zion/
More Power to Ya*
John's Solo: *Jesus
Loves You/The Race*
Bob's Solo
Louie's Solo
*God Gave Rock
and Roll to You*
Praise Medley: *Let
Everything That Hath
Breath/Without Him
We Can Do Nothing/
Praise Ye the Lord/
Hallelujah Chorus*
Godpleaser
The Great I Am
It Is Finished

Petra's only live album to date, *Captured in Time and Space* is a chronicle of the "Beat the System" tour. The recording is very "live" with very few "fixes" afterwards. It also marks the last recording of Greg X. Volz with Petra, as he left shortly after to pursue a solo career. Recorded mainly in Greenville, South Carolina, the audience was wonderful and the band had one of the most memorable concerts ever.

BEAT THE SYSTEM

"Do not conform any longer to the pattern of this world, but be transformed by the renewing of your mind. Then you will be able to test and approve what God's will is—his good, pleasing and perfect will."

Romans 12:2

Beat the System

Words and music by Bob Hartman
© 1984 by Dawn Treader Music/SESAC (a division of Star Song). All rights reserved. International copyright secured. Used by permission.

Caught in the undertow, being swept
downstream—going against the flow
seems like such a dream.
Trying to hold your ground when
you start to slide, pressure to
compromise comes from every side.
Wise up, rise up.
Wise up, rise up.

Chorus
You can be more than a conqueror,
you will never face defeat.
You can dare to win by losing all,
you can face the heat—
dare to beat the system.

On the assembly line, trying to break
the mold, time to throw the
wrench that will stop it cold.
Going against the odds, being the
underdog, dare to wield
the sword that will slice the fog.

Repeat chorus

You can go for it all,
you can go for broke.
You can turn the tide around.
You can aim for the top
and take the lion's share
if you dare to hold your ground.

Repeat chorus

The "system" in this song is the status quo. It is the well-traveled wide path that leads to destruction, for "there is a way that seems right to a man, but in the end it leads to death" (Proverbs 14:12). It is the undertow that sweeps us downstream. How do we as Christians keep from being pulled in directions we know are wrong when it is so easy to follow the crowd? Someone once said that it is easy for a fish to swim downstream, but it takes a fish with real backbone to swim upstream.

Many have asked, "How can I win my friends to the Lord if I don't hang out with them?" Being separate is to be apart from them in your heart. The key is found in Romans 12:2. This verse contains a contrast between the words "conform" and "transformed." The word conform means that our outward actions express our inward nature. In Christ, we have a new nature that is in contradiction to the pattern of this world. Instead we are to be transformed, which means "transfigured," as in the transfiguration of Christ, where His true inner nature was allowed to be seen by Peter, James and John. In other words, we are to outwardly show what has happened to us inside.

Our friends need to see by our actions that our hearts have been changed. It takes courage to act differently and go against the flow. Do you dare to beat the system?

Of all the tours I have been a part of in my 15 years with Petra, Beat the System brings back the greatest memories. After many concerts in the early years with small crowds, it hardly seemed possible that, four years later, we were playing to 8-10,000 people in Las Cruces, New Mexico.

That night I was reminded of the responsibility God had given us in ministry. I had the flu and could hardly walk—much less play the drums. But with God's strength, I knew I could carry on. I had seen other artists play for lesser reasons. Not Petra, not me—but God! One of the guys in our road crew, Jeff Gallup, just picked me up and carried me to the drums. He set me there and said, "I'll be back to get you at the end of the night!" We taped that night and I still watch the concert to remember how God uses us in spite of our physical and mental limitations.

—Louie Weaver

CLEAN

"Jesus answered, ' A person who has had a bath needs only to wash his feet; his whole body is clean. And you are clean.'" — John 13:10

Clean

You might see me stumble, you might see me fall, you might see me cornered with my back against the wall; maybe incognito, maybe out to lunch, maybe caught red-handed or maybe just a hunch.

Chorus
But I'm clean, clean, clean before my Lord, clean, clean, clean before my Lord. Like a spotless lamb I'm blameless in His sight with no trace of wrong left or right, I'm clean, clean, clean.

Kneeling in the closet, begging daily bread, there may be a skeleton hanging overhead. Where are my accusers? Nowhere to be found, they all dropped their stones when the Master came around.

Repeat chorus

I've missed the mark, I can't deny it. I don't condone or justify it. But I've done nothing that His blood can't wash away when I take it to the cross and start to pray.

Repeat chorus

John 13 gives us the account of Jesus washing the disciples' feet. Verse seven lets us know that there was more meaning to this than met the eye. This foot-washing graphically illustrated God's cleansing. I imagine that you and I would react as Peter did when he said with embarrassment, "'Lord, are you going to wash my feet?'" Jesus told Peter that if He didn't wash his feet, Peter would have no part with Him. In Peter's impetuous way, he told Jesus to wash the rest of him as well. Peter wanted all there was to have of Jesus! But Jesus told him, "'A person who has had a bath needs only to wash his feet.'"

What Jesus was trying to tell His disciples has meaning for all believers beyond the message that the greatest is the servant of all. When Jesus "took off his outer clothing," He depicted for us Philippians 2:6, 7, "Who, being in very nature God, did not consider equality with God something to be grasped, but made himself nothing, taking the very nature of a servant, being made in human likeness."

This illustration points directly to the cross where His blood washes us completely from sin. This is the "bath" that Peter wanted! But even after a bath, our feet still get "dirty" while walking in this world. This cleansing comes through our daily confession. This is how we maintain our fellowship with Him.

Spend some time today praising Jesus for the daily cleansing He has provided for you through His blood. His cleansing is for our past, our present and our future, so that we might say as this song does, "I'm clean!"

VOICE IN THE WIND

"'The wind blows wherever it pleases. You hear its sound, but you cannot tell where it comes from or where it is going. So it is with everyone born of the Spirit.'"   *John 3:8*

Voice in the Wind

Wind may come, wind may go,
where it blows no one knows.
Chill the bone, fan the fire,
lead the soul to heart's desire.

Chorus
There's a voice in the wind
that calls your name.
If you listen you'll never be the same.
There's a voice in the wind
that points the way,
gently beckons to follow and obey.

Spirit comes, Spirit goes,
whence it comes no one knows,
breathing life, making new,
filling hearts, calling you.

There's a voice in the wind
that calls your name.
If you listen you'll never be the same.
There's a voice in the wind
that points the way,
gently beckons to follow and obey.

One day when my wife and I were dating, I thought it would be a great romantic afternoon to go sailing. I had never been sailing, but I thought, "What could be so hard? You just catch the wind and aim the boat!" So we rented a small sailboat and set out from the dock while onlookers shook their heads. It was a beautiful sunny day, my future wife looked gorgeous and I was ready to take the credit for an incredible afternoon.

We lacked only one thing: wind. I turned the sail every direction it would move, but still there was nothing. So we drifted. And drifted . . . Then it dawned on me it might not be so easy to get back. So we paddled. And paddled . . .

After thirty minutes, which seemed like a lifetime, we finally reached the dock. Onlookers shook their heads again.

That day I learned an embarrassing lesson about the mystery of wind. You never know where it will blow, or how hard it will blow—or if it will blow at all! To this mystery, Christ compared being born of the Spirit. We can see the effects of the wind. We can hear its sound, or "voice," but we can't see it.

This song was inspired by this mystery. The wind of God's Spirit blows through our hearts. It gently beckons us to follow and obey. Sometimes it's easy to know where it's taking us. Other times, we don't understand the direction it is leading us in. Occasionally, we don't see its effects much at all. But when we listen closely, there is a voice in the wind.

When the Spirit of God directs your course, be sensitive to His leading. Be still and wait on Him, and you will recognize His voice.

The year was 1985, excitement was in the air, my brother John (a new believer) was singing for the group Kansas, and "Fight Fire With Fire" was the #1 rock song in the country. We never wanted it to end . . . then it happened! Kerry Livgren and Dave Hope (also new believers) were excited as well. They had discovered something revolutionary—Christian rock! The music was palatable as well as lyrically bold, music for the Lord. Wow!!

We were hearing names like Petra, Rez Band and Sweet Comfort—pioneers with a message, and suddenly, they became cooler than what we were doing. Petra, the name that seemed to stick with us, became the topic of many of our conversations. Nothing seemed fancy, flashy or musically superior about them. So why all the hoopla?
—Dino Elefante

HOLLOW EYES

" For I was hungry and you gave me something to eat, I was thirsty and you gave me something to drink, I was a stranger and you invited me in, I needed clothes and you clothed me, I was sick and you looked after me, I was in prison and you came to visit me.'"
Matthew 25:35, 36

Hollow Eyes

Words and music by Bob Hartman
© 1984 Dawn Treader Music/SESAC (a division of Star Song). All rights reserved. International copyright secured. Used by permission.

Another day in Nigeria the children beg for bread, the crops failed, the well ran dry when they lost the watershed. A baby dies, its mother cries, the children gather 'round. They're wondering what the day will bring— will they be the next one found?

Chorus
Do you dare to gaze into their hollow eyes? Are they staring holes in you with their hollow eyes?

In the crowded sheds the children lay their heads to escape the Haitian heat. The hunger pains drive them to the street, wondering if today they'll eat. Some find food in the refuse heap, others find disease, some find it harder just to live when they can die with ease.

Repeat chorus

The least of these is hungry, the least of these is sick, the least of these needs clothing, the least of these needs drink, the least of these knows sorrow, the least of these knows grief, the least of these has suffered pain and Jesus is His name.

Do you dare to gaze into His hollow eyes? Is He staring back at you with His hollow eyes?

Petra has had the privilege of working with a wonderful mission organization, called Compassion International, since the early '80s. It means a lot to us that thousands of children in third-world countries have been sponsored as a result of Petra's work. In 1985, my wife and I had the tremendous opportunity to travel to Haiti to meet the little girl we sponsor. Even though they prepared us for what we would see, the depth of poverty that exists in what has been called the "fourth-world" country of Haiti is staggering.

When we finally reached the little village outside of Port-au-Prince where

Rose Marie lives, we had seen enough poverty for a lifetime. My wife and I will never forget how her face lit up when the translator told her we were her sponsors. As I held her for a picture, I noticed how thin she was. Even with the meal she received through Compassion at her school, she was still malnourished. We wanted to give her twenty dollars for her birthday, but they told us to give her no more than ten because she wouldn't be able to comprehend how anyone could be rich enough to give away twenty dollars.

I suddenly realized what it means to be rich and what it means to be poor. In America, we simply do not understand how rich and blessed we are. The abundant Scriptures concerning the poor make it crystal clear that we have a responsibility to help meet their needs.

When we give, we are giving to Christ Himself. As we gaze into the "hollow eyes" of poverty, I hope you and I will see the One who is really looking back at us: the Man of Sorrows, Jesus Christ.

PETRASPECTIVE 1986-1988

Back to the Street (1989)

Song List

Back to the Street
You Are I Am
Shakin' the House
King's Ransom
Whole World
Another Crossroad
Run for Cover
Fools Gold
Altar Ego
Thankful Heart

This album featured a new singer, John Schlitt, as well as new producers—John and Dino Elefante. It was bound to be drastically different from the start. With the more rocky character of John's voice, the production followed suit with an intentional return to the hard rock of our earlier recordings. John had not been singing for five years and his voice was a little rusty but very true to his roots.

Radio warmly received "Thankful Heart," which marked the first of many successful collaborations of songwriting with the Elefantes. The changes we made breathed new life into the band and set the tone for the next several recordings.

This Means War! (1987)

Song List

This Means War!

*He Came, He Saw,
He Conquered*

*Get on Your Knees
and Fight Like a Man*

I Am Available

Kenaniah

You Are My Rock

The Water Is Alive

*Don't Let Your
Heart Be Hardened*

Dead Reckoning

All the King's Horses

I consider this recording to be a great turning point for the group because it firmly established the new sound. Again we were very successful at Christian radio with "Don't Let Your Heart Be Hardened," as well as the title song and one of our all-time greatest concert songs, "He Came, He Saw, He Conquered." The lyrics were very thematic, focusing mainly on spiritual warfare.

John's voice was much more seasoned after touring and his performance was noticeably improved. Also the sophomore effort with John and Dino, the working relationship in the studio was much smoother and resulted in a much more cohesive sound. The tour came alive and the message of spiritual warfare was embraced by many.

On Fire! (1988)

Song List

All Fired Up

Hit You Where You Live

Mine Field

First Love

Defector

Counsel of the Holy

Somebody's Gonna Praise His Name

Open Book

Stand in the Gap

Homeless Few

As *Not of This World* was a sequel to *More Power to Ya*, *On Fire!* was the follow-up to *This Means War!* "First Love" hit at radio and "All Fired Up" and "Hit You Where You Live" became concert mainstays. We were excited to realize that we were reaching an entirely new audience with our music—a decidedly younger audience.

THANKFUL HEART

"So then, just as you received Christ Jesus as Lord, continue to live in him, rooted and built up in him, strengthened in the faith as you were taught, and overflowing with thankfulness." Colossians 2:6, 7

Thankful Heart

Words by Bob Hartman and Dino Elefante
Music by John Elefante
© 1986 Dawn Treader Music/SESAC (a division of Star Song), Petsong Publishing/SESAC (admin. by Gaither Copyright Management) and Uncle Pitts Publishing/BMI. All rights reserved. International copyright secured. Used by permission.

Chorus
I have a thankful heart that you have given me and it can only come from you.

There is no way to begin to tell you how I feel, there are no words to express how you've become so real.
Jesus, you've given me so much I can't repay, I have no offering.

Repeat chorus

There is no way to begin to tell you how I feel. There's nothing more I can say and no way to repay Your warming touch that melts my heart of stone, Your steadfast love—I'll never be alone.

Repeat chorus
I have a thankful heart, words don't come easily but I am sure you can see my thankful heart.

Help me be a man of God, a man who's after Your own heart, help me show my gratitude and keep in me a thankful heart.

As a child, when someone would give me something, my mother would remind me, "What do you say?" I would then muster a belated "Thank you." Now, as, a father, I say the same thing to my son. My hope is to cultivate more than just good manners. My desire is that he will grow to have a thankful heart. In a Christian, thankfulness is not etiquette; it is humility before God when faced with the truth of our standing in Him. To understand and appreciate where we are, we must have a grasp on where we have been.

Ephesians 2:12 sums up our former condition with the threefold indictment, "without hope and without God in the world." We were without hope. There was nothing we ourselves could do to improve our condition in any way. We were hopelessly lost. We were without God. Separated by our sin, we had no access or fellowship with Him. And, we were in the world. We were a part of the kingdom of darkness and not the kingdom of light, doomed to the same fate as all evil.

It took a miracle to change our condition. It took God, calling us out of the darkness and into His light, making us His sons and daughters, giving us access to His throne through the blood of Jesus Christ and forever sealing us with His Spirit to live eternally with Him.

The call came . . . from Bob Hartman. He was a quiet man, not a big talker. I don't remember a man ever saying as much to me using so few words! We compared notes musically, spiritually and personally. Bob decided to fly me without John to Nashville to start working out some tunes to see how it felt. The music was going great, John joined us ten days later and we continued in the making of *Back to the Street.*

We were especially excited since it was Petra's first album with vocalist John Schlitt (formerly of the band Head East). We were in our element musically but still didn't quite know what made it all tick, not knowing we would have many more opportunities to find out.

—Dino Elefante

Salvation is the gift of God, so there is no way we can take any credit for it. We must view it every day with the humility that brings forth a thankful heart.

THIS MEANS WAR!

"And there was war in heaven. Michael and his angels fought against the dragon, and the dragon and his angels fought back."   *Revelation 12:7*

This Means War!

Son of the morning, highest of all,
you had so much going till you
took the fall; had a place in the glory,
but you wanted it all, impossible
odds but you had the gall.
It seemed so unlikely that you
would rebel, such a worthy
opponent that you knew so well.
But you went down fighting when
you heard the bell, took a third of all
Heaven when you went to Hell.

Chorus
This means war—and the battle's still
raging, war—and though both sides are
waging, the Victor is sure and the
victory secure but till judgment we all
must endure—this means war!

Then came the cross—you thought
you had won, you thought you
had conquered God's only Son.
"So much for Jesus," you said
in jest. Then you got a visit
from an unwelcome guest.

Repeat chorus

Now it's all over, down to the wire,
counting the days to your own
lake of fire. But you'll go down
fighting for all that you're worth
to try to abolish His image on earth.

Repeat chorus

This song is about Satan's history before Adam and his eventual demise. We live in the time between these events so, as the song says, "till judgment we all must endure." I don't know why God in His wisdom chose to delay the final judgment of Satan. How I wish we didn't have to deal with him, but deal with him we must.

There are a few things about his tactics that are helpful to know. The Bible sums up his threefold attack in this way: "For everything in the world—the cravings of sinful man, the lust of his eyes and the boasting of what he has and does—comes not from the Father but from the world" (1 John 2:16). All of our temptations will fall into one or more of these areas. Satan preys upon these weaknesses in man and even tried to appeal to God's own Son with them in the wilderness. The first weakness is the craving for physical pleasure. Nothing could characterize our modern world better. The second is the weakness of greed. Again, a very contemporary problem. And thirdly, the weakness of pride.

Christ gave us a lesson on how to win these battles by quoting Scripture each time. This is why we must heed what David wrote, "I have hidden your word in my heart that I might not sin against you" (Psalm 119:11). If we know God's Word and have it hidden in our hearts, we will be ready when these times of temptation come.

Satan was completely defeated at Calvary, but there are many battles for you and me while we wait for his final punishment. Jesus was tested in every way that we could be—yet He never sinned. To follow Him is to fight Satan with the power of God's Word. Stand strong, knowing you will ultimately win this war!

HE CAME, HE SAW, HE CONQUERED

"'I am the Living One; I was dead, and behold I am alive for ever and ever! And I hold the keys of death and Hades.'"   *Revelation 1:18*

He Came, He Saw, He Conquered
Words by Bob Hartman
Music by Bob Hartman and John Elefante
© 1987 Dawn Treader Music/SESAC (a division of Star Song), Petsong Publishing/SESAC (admin. by Gaither Copyright Management) and Uncle Pitts Publishing/BMI. All rights reserved. International copyright secured. Used by permission.

He came alone into the battle, He knew nobody else could face His foe. He left His throne, He left His glory, He knew nobody else could ever go. He called the bluff, He took the challenge, He came into this world to seek and save. No one could know, no one could fathom the way to win was only through the grave. They laid Him in His tomb, they thought they'd sealed His doom. But He rose, He rose!

Chorus
He came, He saw, He conquered death and Hell. He came, He saw, He is alive and well. He was, He is, and only He forgives, He died, He rose, He lives. He came, He saw, He conquered!

The doors were locked, they heard Him knocking; they were afraid they would be taken, too. Familiar voices said, "Come and follow," come and see the things the Lord can do. They went to where He lay, the stone was rolled away, He rose, He rose!

Repeat chorus

He came into this world, He saw humanity, He heard the S.O.S., He met the enemy. The enemy was conquered, the enemy was conquered.

Repeat chorus

This victory song is one of my all-time favorites to perform. Many times I can remember sensing the presence of God on stage as John Schlitt proclaimed, "He rose!" I would not be exaggerating to say that the resurrection of Jesus Christ from the dead was the greatest event in human history. It is so important to our faith that the apostle Paul stated, "And if Christ has not been raised, your faith is futile; you are still in your sins" (1 Corinthians 15:17). But He *has* been raised. He arose from the grave. He lives! In fact, He can do nothing less because He is life incarnate! (John 5:26). The grave couldn't possibly hold Him who had the power over His own life (John 10:18).

It is that resurrection life that we receive when we receive Him! And it is His resurrection power that enables us to live for Him (Ephesians 1:19-21). And it will be this power that will raise us up (1 Thessalonians 4:14) and change us to be like Him (Philippians 3:21). It was the resurrection that changed His disciples from frightened men hiding in an upper room to powerful evangelists who turned the world upside down! He can do this for you and me as well.

"Because He lives, I can face tomorrow," as the song says. We can face anything in life because we know that our God lives! He has already conquered everything we will face.

Take time today to think about His resurrection and what it means to you. It is my prayer that you will experience His resurrection power in your life in a very real way.

GET ON YOUR KNEES AND FIGHT LIKE A MAN

"The weapons we fight with are not the weapons of the world. On the contrary, they have divine power to demolish strongholds." **2 Corinthians 10:4**

Get on Your Knees and Fight Like a Man

Out on your own and with your own self-reliance, you've got no one to watch your back. You find yourself caught with no strong alliance, you've been left open for attack.

Over your head the condition is graver; you've given ground you can't retrieve. The cards are stacked and they're not in your favor but you've got an ace up your sleeve.

Chorus
Get on your knees and fight like a man. You'll pull down strongholds if you just believe you can. Your enemy will tuck his tail and flee. Get on your knees and fight like a man.

Under the gun you've got no place to hide out, backed in the corner on your own. This is one storm you are destined to ride out, one way to leave the danger zone.

Repeat chorus

You've got the backbone to fight this tide, you've got the will to survive, you've got the weapon—it's at your side, you've got to learn to confide.

I was raised on TV westerns, where men were men, and they settled things with their fists. Many saloon fights began with the words, "Get on your feet and fight like a man!" After becoming a Christian, I realized that a man is never taller than when he is on his knees. It takes a lot more courage to fight with spiritual weapons on our knees before God than it does to try to fight with earthly "weapons." When conflict comes, we usually try everything else first. We talk to the teacher, tell our boss or complain to our mom. We buy them off, tell them off or flip them off!

God wants us to have a different perspective on conflict. Our conflicts originate in the spiritual realm. "For our struggle is not against flesh and blood, but against the rulers, against the authorities, against the powers of this dark world and against the spiritual forces of evil in the heavenly realms" (Ephesians 6:12). Spiritual warfare necessitates spiritual weapons. It takes greater courage to pray for our "enemies," and then treat them the way Christ would treat them. It becomes easier when we realize that *they* are not the problem! Their actions against us are caused by a deeper spiritual problem. Only when we realize this can we love them enough to pray against that spiritual problem. When that seems like a hopelessly lost cause, we need only remember that God was able to reach our rebellious heart and turn it towards Him. Don't underestimate the power of God through the weapon of prayer!

Do you have a conflict with someone now? Take a moment to use your spiritual weapons and pray for him or her. Get on your knees and fight like a man!

I AM AVAILABLE

"Then I heard the voice of the Lord saying, 'Whom shall I send? And who will go for us?' And I said, 'Here am I. Send me!'"   Isaiah 6:8

I Am Available

Words and music by Bob Hartman
© 1987 Dawn Treader Music/SESAC (a division of Star Song) and Petsong Publishing/SESAC (admin. by Gaither Copyright Management). All rights reserved. International copyright secured. Used by permission.

I don't have much to offer you,
I don't have much to give.
There's so much I may never be
as long as I may live.
And I may never be all I want to be
although I'll always try.
But if you choose me, to use me,
there's just one reason why.

Chorus
I am available, I am available,
I will go when you say, "Go."
I am available, I am available,
I will stop when you say, "No."
My whole life was incomplete
till I laid it at your feet,
So use me as you will, I am available.

I'm not the most dependable—
sometimes you can't rely.
There's no excuse, there is no defense,
there's only one reply.

Repeat chorus

I know that my ability
is not Your main concern,
it's my availability and
willingness to learn.

Repeat chorus

In Isaiah 6 is a beautiful illustration of a man making himself available to God. But if we read the fifth verse of this chapter, we see that something happened that led to this confidence and availability. As Isaiah witnessed the very holiness of God, He became aware of his own sin. He responded, "'I am ruined! For I am a man of unclean lips.'"

Many people don't make themselves available to God for this same reason. We feel unworthy to be used by Him. But as soon as the seraph delivered the message that Isaiah's guilt was taken away and his sin atoned for, he knew that God had made him worthy. We don't need an angel to deliver this message to us because we have the Word of

God, which tells us, "If we confess our sins, he is faithful and just and will forgive us our sins and purify us from all unrighteousness" (1 John 1:9).

Another reason many people don't make themselves available is that they feel inadequate. In Exodus 4:10, when God called Moses to deliver the Israelites from Egypt, Moses said, "'O Lord, I have never been eloquent, neither in the past nor since you have spoken to your servant. I am slow of speech and tongue.'" Moses thought God had made a mistake and should have chosen someone who was better at speaking. But God doesn't make mistakes. The Bible is filled with stories of ordinary men who did extraordinary things because God was with them.

God is more interested in our availability than our ability. He has been able to use Petra in spite of the fact that we feel unworthy and inadequate. How about you? I hope that we can inspire you to make yourself available to God.

DON'T LET YOUR HEART BE HARDENED

"But encourage one another daily, as long as it is called Today, so that none of you may be hardened by sin's deceitfulness." — *Hebrews 3:13*

Don't Let Your Heart Be Hardened

Chorus
Don't let your heart be hardened,
don't let your love grow cold.
May it always stay so childlike,
may it never grow too old.
Don't let your heart be hardened,
may you always know the cure.
Keep it broken before Jesus;
keep it thankful, meek, and pure.

May it always feel compassion,
may it beat as one with God's.
May it never be contrary,
may it never be at odds.
May it always be forgiving,
may it never know conceit.
May it always be encouraged,
may it never know defeat.

Repeat chorus

May your heart be always open,
never satisfied with right.
May your heart be filled with courage
and be strengthened with all might.
Let His love rain down upon you,
breaking up your fallow ground;
Let it loosen all the binding,
till only tenderness is found.

Repeat chorus

I wrote this song shortly after John Schlitt joined the band. He was so full of innocence and zeal, having been out of music altogether for five years following his conversion to Christ. John knew nothing of the frustrations of being an artist in the Christian music business. Unfortunately, I have seen those frustrations turn many hearts cold, bitter and cynical toward the things of God. But John's heart was fresh, and his infectious enthusiasm was apparent in every interview and every performance. I wanted it to stay that way!

Hardness of heart comes from sin in our lives—and it doesn't happen overnight. Sin is deceitful. At first, we are repentant, but then we sin again and we feel defeated. Then we begin to rationalize and blame others. Next, we begin to feel resentful towards others who seem to have their lives together, so we withdraw from fellowship, and suddenly, we are right where the devil wants us: alone and defeated, bitter and cynical. The longer we stay there, the harder our hearts grow toward God. When we do not remain in a place where others can encourage us, we have played right into the devil's hand.

I thank God that John's heart is still warm and open to the things of God. How about you? Where are you in this process? Don't be deceived! Don't separate yourself from the fellowship that brings encouragement. Don't let your heart be hardened!

As my brother and I observed the members of Petra, the picture soon became clear. Though the usual problems of meshing five distinctly different personalities and talents existed, their priority was evident—to reach the youth of the church.

As Christian music picked up steam, image became the benchmark for many artists, sometimes overshadowing the message. The first time my brother and I felt that God had called us to be part of this ministry—not just be employed by it—was when we shared Petra's pain in repeatedly being overlooked for awards.

But Petra kept its eyes on the youth, in their relentless commitment to serve. With loving hearts, they sacrificed far too often friendships, wives and families to be with kids, to pray with them, hug them and perform for them. It suddenly hit us—it's not about the music, the awards, the recognition, the affirmation. But the message. The message. The message!

—Dino Elefante

HIT YOU WHERE YOU LIVE

"No discipline seems pleasant at the time, but painful. Later on, however, it produces a harvest of righteousness and peace for those who have been trained by it."
Hebrews 12:11

Hit You Where You Live

You want to change with all your might,
you want to do right in His sight.
It's His delight to give you your desire,
it's His desire to set your life on fire.
Sometimes it hurts when reprimanded,
it hurts Him more than it's hurtin' you.
He'll pick you up from where you
landed, when He knocks you down,
turns your life around.

Chorus
Hit you where you live, you can't hold it
back. When you're struck by His love
you will know. Hit you where you live,
it's so close to home. When you're all
sold out the mark will show.
Let Him hit you where you live.

The evidence leads to conviction
when we don't live everything we say.
There's got to be a crucifixion,
we can live dying every day.
You've got to tell Him He's
free to take a shot. He wants to
hit you with everything He's got.

Repeat chorus

A lost and dying world is
dying to know He lives.
The only way they'll know
what He has to give
is when we're hit where we live.

People always told me I would learn much about the Lord by becoming a parent. When I became one, I discovered how right they were! Disciplining a child is one of the hardest things I have ever done. I love my son so much and I want him to be happy all the time. I feel the most fulfilled as a father when he is smiling and laughing. But I also know that his long-term happiness is much more complicated. He must be taught what is right and wrong in the eyes of God and other people if he is to be a well-adjusted and happy adult.

As his father, I am given the awesome responsibility of "training" him. It is a painful process for both father and son! I tell him that I can't be the kind of father

God wants me to be if I don't discipline him.

This process has helped me to understand the discipline of God, which is the subject of "Hit You Where You Live." Hebrews 12:6 tells us that God disciplines those He loves. I personally believe that, just as a parent of more than one child will discipline each child a little differently, God disciplines His children uniquely as well. Through something a friend says, or a Scripture we read or a message we hear, we know when God is reaching into our hearts and putting His finger on something that displeases Him. We know when He has "hit us where we live," and it hurts. It is evidence of God's loving fatherhood and His desire to "train" us.

When this happens to you, don't lose heart! If you allow Him to change you, it will produce a harvest of righteousness and peace in your life!

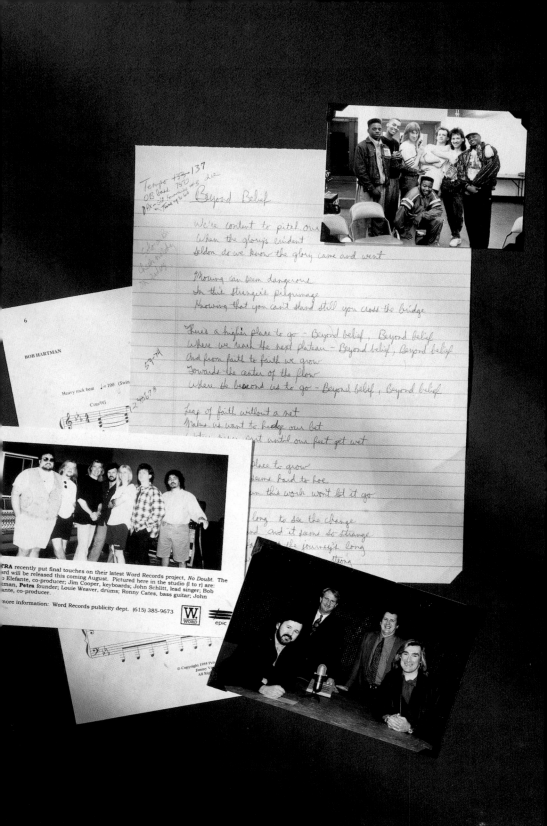

Tempo ♩=137
OB lead 75▢ #3 Lie
DB ...

Beyond Belief

We're content to pitch our ...
When the glory's evident
Seldom do we know the glory came and went

Moving can seem dangerous
In this stranger's pilgrimage
Knowing that you can't stand still you cross the bridge

There's a higher place to go - Beyond belief, Beyond belief
Where we reach the next plateau - Beyond belief, Beyond belief
And from faith to faith we grow
Towards the center of the flow
Where He beacons us to go - Beyond belief, Beyond belief

Leap of faith without a net
Makes us want to hedge our bet
... until our feet get wet

... place to grow
... seems hard to hoe
... this work won't let it go

... long, to see the change
... and it seems so strange
... the journey's long
... strong

6

BOB HARTMAN

Heavy rock beat ♩=100 (Swin...

Cmaj9/G

2 3 4 5 6 7 8

59 74

© Copyright 1993 Pet...
Jimmy V...
All Rig...

PETRA recently put final touches on their latest Word Records project, *No Doubt*. The ... ard will be released this coming August. Pictured here in the studio (l to r) are: ...o Elefante, co-producer; Jim Cooper, keyboards; John Schlitt, lead singer; Bob ...eman, **Petra** founder; Louie Weaver, drums; Ronny Cates, bass guitar; John ...ante, co-producer.

...nore information: Word Records publicity dept. (615) 385-9673

W. WORD   epic

Grammy & Dove award-winning group Petra has re-signed an exclusive recording agreement with Word Records. The signing was held at Nashville's Hard Rock Cafe, where much of the group's memorabilia is displayed. The Hard R... ...cated the event by presenting the group with jackets, displayed here by Petra me... ...igning, are l to r: (back row) John Schlitt, Petra; Lynn Keesecker, gene... president, Word Records & Music; Louie Wea... Hartman, founder, Petra; Ronnie Cates, Petra... ...land Lundy,

MINE FIELD

> *"He must also have a good reputation with outsiders, so that he will not fall into disgrace and into the devil's trap."*
>
> *1 Timothy 3:7*

Mine Field

Smell the burning powder?
There's danger in the air.
A voice from deep inside is telling you,
"You must beware." The enemy is
watching every step you take to find his
opportunity in every choice you make.
And it's no game when someone lives
without His grace. And who's to blame
when it blows up in their face?

Chorus
It's a mine field—you'd better follow
Him through. God knows the way you'd
better stick like glue. It's a mine field—
better stay on His heels 'cause the
enemy kills and the enemy steals. So keep
your head down and keep your eyes
peeled 'cause life is, life is a mine field.

Think the grass is greener?
You'd better look around.
Everywhere you look another casualty is
found. The enemy is waiting for you to
start to run, waiting like an itchy finger
on a loaded gun. And some may feel they
can wander out too far. They may heal
but they may always wear the scar.

Repeat chorus

Better leave the navigation to
the One who knows the Way.
He will bring illumination,
He will light your path each day.

Repeat chorus
Better watch where you tread, step off
the path and you could end up dead.

Any foot soldier knows the dangers of a land mine. You could be walking along, thinking everything is fine, when all of a sudden—boom! One false step is all it takes. Life is a mine field. There are dangers for the Christian in every step. Maybe we shouldn't be out front leading the way. Wouldn't it be safer to follow the One who has been through the field already, and knows where to step? That's why God wants to lead us in making the right choices.

In the army, if you don't follow the commands of your leader, you or someone else could end up dead. Our leader, God, gives the Christian soldier commands as well. Many Christians have been "killed" or "maimed" from not following these commands. God gives us commandments to protect us. If we disobey, many times we pay a bitter price. The second verse of this song speaks of those who "wander out too far. They may heal but they may always wear the scar." I have made many mistakes in my Christian life. I often wish I could go back in time and warn myself. But I did have a warning: God's Word.

We need to heed His warnings so that we don't end up spending years trying to unwind problems which result when we step out from under God's protective umbrella, His commandments. Jesus knows every one of the devil's traps. He knows the way through the mine field of life. All we have to do is follow.

Do you, or someone you know, have any "scars" from wandering out too far from His commands— things that have long since been forgiven, but the scars of those past mistakes remain? Save yourself the scars by following the only One who knows the way through the mine field.

FIRST LOVE

> *"'Yet I hold this against you: You have forsaken your first love.'"* — *Revelation 2:4*

First Love

Words by Bob Hartman
Music by John Elefante
© Copyright 1988 by Petsong Publishing/SESAC
(admin. by Word, Inc.) and Uncle Pitts
Publishing/BMI. All rights reserved. International
copyright secured. Used by permission.

Sometimes I feel I'm pulled
in so many wrong directions,
sometimes I feel the world
seducing my affections.
It's not that I don't know the way,
it's just a heart that's prone to stray,
but with my weaknesses admitted,
you will keep all that I've committed
so I commit my heart to You,
my first love.

Chorus
First love, first love,
my soul longs after You.
First love, my first love,
I want my heart to stay so true.
Because You first loved me,
Jesus, You will always be,
You will always be my first love.

It's taken me some time
to try to comprehend
a love that doesn't change,
a love without an end,
a love that keeps forgiving,
a love of sacrifice and giving.
I delight myself in You,
my first love.

Repeat chorus

If I ever lack endurance
I remember Your assurance,
that Your only banner over me is love.
If my heart begins to waiver,
woo me back, my loving Savior,
woo me back till I return
to my first love.

Repeat chorus

This verse from Revelation was written to the angel of the church at Ephesus. Without trying to speculate who had forsaken their first love, there is still a great lesson for us in this portion of Scripture. If we read the preceding verses, it appears as if these people were doing everything right. They worked hard, stood by the truth and endured hardships. But something was still missing. In their hearts, they had left their first love. They were a church just going through the motions. They had all the outward appearances but they lacked the reality and the "heart" of Christian worship. They lacked love for Jesus Christ.

The message to us is clear. We can appear to be doing everything right even though our Christianity has become an

empty ritual. God hates empty ritual.
Sometimes we remember the "how to" but
we forget the "why." Christianity is based on
a love relationship with Christ, and when
that love grows cold or stale, we have fallen
away. Thank God, the next verse gives us the
cure: "'Repent and do the things you did at
first.'" *Repent* means to go in another direction. In this context, that direction is back to
doing the things we did at first.

Remember how vibrant your relationship
with Christ was when you first became a
Christian? How you seemed to fall more in
love with your Savior each and every day?
This is how God wants us to be every day.

*Someone once told me that one of the most revealing
questions a person can ask himself is: "Was there ever
a time when I was more in love with the Lord than I
am today?" If you and I have to answer "yes" to that
question, we need to return to our first love.*

Petra Praise . . . The Rock Cries Out (1989)

Song List

I Love the Lord

Kings of Kings

Jesus, Jesus, Glorious One

The Battle Belongs to the Lord

Take Me In

Salvation Belongs to Our God

The King of Glory Shall Come In

No Weapon Formed Against Us

I Will Celebrate/When the Spirit of the Lord

I Will Sing Praise

Hallowed Be Thy Name

Friends (All in the Family of God)

I Will Call Upon the Lord

We Exalt Thee

At our new home with Word Records, we did something very different: a rock praise record! No one knew, including us, how our fans would respond to such a different record. The idea came from youth pastors who expressed a need for praise songs. The songs were our versions of popular choruses being sung in churches across the country with the exception of a couple of original songs, one of which became a concert favorite—"I Love the Lord."

"I Will Call Upon the Lord" and "We Exalt Thee" were already a part of our concerts. The album made them even more popular with our audiences. Petra Praise . . . The Rock Cries Out continues to be one of our best-selling records and we attribute that to the spirit of praise and worship that went into its recording.

Beyond Belief (1990)

Song List

Armed and Dangerous
I Am on the Rock
Creed
Beyond Belief
Love
Underground
Seen and Not Heard
Last Daze
What's in a Name
Prayer

This album continues to be a favorite of both our fans and the group members. Everything seemed to come together on this record. The working relationship with the producers, the songwriting, the excellent job done by the record company and, of course, the response of the fans.

"Prayer" and "Love," as well as "Beyond Belief," "Armed and Dangerous" and "Seen and Not Heard" received heavy airplay. Combined with the tour with Josh McDowell and the *Beyond Belief* video, all the pistons seemed to be firing at once. This is our biggest selling record to date.

Unseen Power (1991)

Song List

Destiny
Who's on the Lord's Side
Ready, Willing and Able
Hand on My Heart
I Need to Hear From You
Dance
Secret Weapon
Sight Unseen
Hey World
In the Likeness of You

Riding on the heels of the success of *Beyond Belief* came *Unseen Power*. By this time, the recording process with John and Dino was beginning to feel somewhat mechanical. We all knew it, so we set out to intentionally go about things differently. Regrettably, the record was rushed in both its conceptualization and its production. Neil Kernon was hired to mix and did a superb job of achieving a huge sound. The band attempted to play and sing differently from any previous record.

There wasn't much for Christian radio, but "Hand on My Heart" was very well received and "Dance" did well with radio and in concert. We knew we needed to shift our direction, but like an ocean liner, it's not always easy to make a sharp turn. I see *Unseen Power* as a transitional step.

ARMED AND DANGEROUS

"Put on the full armor of God so that you can take your stand against the devil's schemes."
Ephesians 6:11

Armed and Dangerous
Words and music by Bob Hartman
© 1990 by Petsong Publishing/SESAC.
All rights reserved. Used by permission.

It used to be a distant call,
thought to be for some but never all.
Now our wounded lay on every side,
now this call to arms can't be denied.
The enemy will tremble as young and
old assemble, a mighty army up in arms.

Chorus
Armed and dangerous, God's enemies
will scatter. Armed and dangerous, we'll
see the darkness shatter. His armor is
worth its weight, no weapon can
penetrate. Armed and dangerous,
we're ready to storm the gate.

We're not so tough on our own, no one
can even stand all alone. Just a ragtag
army at its best, we sometimes even fail
the smallest test. But through this
tribulation there comes a transforma-
tion, we don the armor of our King.

Repeat chorus

Stand up against the flood,
stand, covered by His blood.
We are the standard He has raised.
Stand, earnestly contend,
stand to the very end.
We've only just begun to fight!

Repeat chorus

Being chained to a Roman guard made it easy for Paul to analogize about the armor of God. In this song I wanted to communicate that not only are we soldiers equipped with armor (2 Timothy 2:3), we are also a potential "nightmare" for the enemy!

It's hard for us to think in terms of fighting. It goes against the grain of our peaceful instincts. Maybe that's why so many Christians have been decimated by the attacks of the enemy. I hoped that this song would make us aware that spiritual warfare is a daily fact in the Christian's walk with God. We need to heed 1 Peter 5:8: "Be self-controlled and alert. Your enemy the devil prowls around like a roaring lion looking for someone to devour."

Why is Satan so bent on the destruction of Christians? Much as the jilted girl destroys the picture or "image" of her former boyfriend, Satan seeks to destroy the image of the one he hates the most. That One is "Christ in you, the hope of glory." We are His image in this world. God is at work in this world through His Church and the enemy seeks to destroy that work. His goal is to make us ineffective Christians.

Jesus said that Satan came to "steal and kill and destroy" (John 10:10). No doubt you can think of several Christians who have become part of Satan's statistics. Don't let it happen to you! And pray for others. Know how to use the "sword of the Spirit, which is the word of God" (Ephesians 6: 17).

Don't be caught sitting on your armor. Put it on. Use it. There is nothing Satan fears more than a soldier of Jesus who knows how to use the weapons at his disposal. Face each day, with the realization that, while wearing the armor of God and walking in His Spirit, you are "armed and dangerous"!

I AM ON THE ROCK

"'Therefore everyone who hears these words of mine and puts them into practice is like a wise man who built his house on the rock.'" Matthew 7:24

I Am on the Rock

The earth is shakin', it's like a bad
dream. This world is crumblin',
comin' apart at the seam, but
I am on the Rock, I am on the Rock.

Everywhere I'm turning it's only bad
news. This bomb is tickin' and we're
getting to the end of the fuse, but
I am on the Rock, I am on the Rock.

Chorus
I am on the Rock, the sure foundation,
I am on the Rock, His revelation.
Though the winds may blow and
though the floods may grow
I shall not be moved, 'cause
I am on the Rock.

The storm's approaching,
I'm standing high and dry,
Firmly planted on the Rock
that is higher than I,
I am on the Rock,
I am on the Rock.

Kingdoms failing, they fall around
me, plans eroded, and
washing away to the sea.
I am on the Rock,
I am on the Rock.

Repeat chorus

There is no Rock in this
world but our God.

During the recording of *Beyond Belief*, I was in California working in the studio. One day, while sitting in the lounge talking to my wife on the phone, I felt a very weird sensation. There was a low rumbling sound as if someone were moving heavy furniture nearby. Suddenly, it seemed like the floor of the building began to move in an almost circular motion. I said to my wife, "We're having an earthquake!" Being from Tennessee, I was not accustomed to anything that resembled that feeling. I'm sure it lasted less than a minute, but it seemed like much longer.

I remember the feeling of disorientation I had afterward. When I walked, I felt off balance. I felt the need to grab something to steady me. I began to realize that all my life I had perceived the ground to be a stable point of reference. Everything that moved was in contrast to the ground which stood still. In less than a minute, my perception was altered. For a brief moment, nothing was stable.

Later, after things returned to "normal," I received a great spiritual lesson from this experience. If we could see this world the way God does, we would realize that everything is "unstable" but Him! Everything we see and know is temporal, but He is eternal. And if we build our lives on Him, the rains, floods—yes, even the earthquakes of life— cannot move us! All other ground is shifting sand.

Every day we build a little more on this edifice we call our "life." Have you asked yourself, "What am I building on?" He is our Rock and He doesn't change. Can you say, "I am on the Rock"?

28

CREED

"So then, brothers, stand firm and hold to the teachings we passed on to you, whether by word of mouth or by letter." **2 Thessalonians 2:15**

Creed
Words and music by Bob Hartman
© 1990 by Petsong Publishing/SESAC.
All rights reserved. Used by permission.

I believe in God the Father, Maker of Heaven and earth and in Jesus Christ, His only Son, I believe in the virgin birth. I believe in the Man of Sorrows bruised for iniquities, I believe in the Lamb who was crucified and hung between two thieves.

I believe in the resurrection on the third and glorious day, and I believe in the empty tomb and the stone that the angel rolled away. He descended and set the captives free and now He sits at God's right hand and prepares a place for me.

Chorus
This is my creed—the witness I have heard, the faith that has endured, this truth is assured. Through the darkest ages past, though persecuted, it will last and I will hold steadfast to this creed.

I believe He sent His Spirit to comfort and to reveal, to lead us into truth and light, to baptize and to seal. I believe that He will come back the way He went away and receive us all unto Himself, but no man knows the day.

Repeat chorus

I believe He is the Judge of all men, small and great. The resurrected souls of men receive from Him their fate—some to death and some to life, some to their reward, some to sing eternal praise forever to our Lord.

I grew up in a church that recited the Apostles' Creed every Sunday. Unfortunately, the church didn't believe in a personal relationship with Christ. A couple of years after I quit going, I invited Christ into my life and I was born again. Even though it meant little to me at the time, the Apostles' Creed stuck in my memory and I gained a great appreciation for it after I came to know Christ as my personal Savior.

The idea to write this song came from an off-the-cuff comment made by my wife. She said, "I would like to see you write a song about what we believe as Christians." The first thing that came to my mind was the Apostles' Creed. I started to realize that Christians for centuries have recited this creed as a statement of their faith and it has been faithfully passed down and guarded from generation to generation. Men and women have lost their lives for believing this creed. It is part of our great heritage in the faith.

Paul exhorted the Thessalonians to "hold to the teachings we passed on to you." I want this song to be a part of passing this faith on to the next generation. Since we began playing it in concert, it has become one of our most requested songs. Below is the Apostles' Creed in its entirety. As you read it, think about how important the Truth really is. It is the Truth that sets us free. Join with your fellow believers in embracing it as your own.

I believe in God, the Father almighty, Creator of Heaven and earth. I believe in Jesus Christ, His only Son, our Lord. He was conceived by the power of the Holy Spirit and born of the virgin Mary. He suffered under Pontius Pilate, was crucified, died, and was buried. He descended into Hell. On the third day He rose again. He ascended into Heaven, and is seated at the right hand of the Father. He will come again to judge the living and the dead. I believe in the Holy Spirit, the holy Christian church, the communion of saints, the forgiveness of sins, the resurrection of the body, and the life everlasting. Amen.

BEYOND BELIEF

"Brothers, I do not consider myself yet to have taken hold of it. But one thing I do: Forgetting what is behind and straining toward what is ahead, I press on toward the goal to win the prize for which God has called me heavenward in Christ Jesus."

Philippians 3:13, 14

Beyond Belief

Words and music by Bob Hartman
© 1990 by Petsong Publishing/SESAC.
All rights reserved. Used by permission.

We're content to pitch our tent when the glory's evident, seldom do we know the glory came and went. Moving can seem dangerous in this stranger's pilgrimage, knowing that you can't stand still, you cross the bridge.

Chorus
There's a higher place to go—
beyond belief, beyond belief,
where we reach the next plateau—
beyond belief, beyond belief.
And from faith to faith we grow
towards the center of the flow
where He beckons us to go—
beyond belief, beyond belief.

Leap of faith without a net makes us want to hedge our bet, waters never part until our feet get wet. There's a deeper place to go where the road seems hard to hoe. He who has begun this work won't let it go.

Repeat chorus

And it takes so long to see the change but we look around and it seems so strange. We have come so far, but the journey's long, and we once were weak but now we're strong.

Repeat chorus

This song is about pressing on, past the point at which we first believed and on to knowing and walking with Christ in a deeper way. There is no end to how far we can go in our relationship with Him, yet there are those who trust Christ for their salvation and go no further. The point of salvation is just the beginning of an incredible journey.

Early in my Christian life I was told that if salvation is all there is, God should take us on home right then. He has plans for us in this life and the next. His main design is to mold us into the image of His Son so that His glory might be revealed in us (Romans 8:18, 29).

Here in Philippians, Paul compares this process to a runner straining with all his energies toward the finish line. We too should press on to the end of the race. Often we reach a place of contentment and want to "pitch our tent" and remain there. But God desires for us to be mobile and ready to follow Him anywhere at any time. His timing is perfect, so, unless we are plugged in, we may miss the next exciting turn in this race.

I am convinced that God likes change. It's what keeps us out of a rut. Over the span of Petra's ministry, there have been many changes. I used to be fearful each time a new one came along. But I have learned that God can be trusted with what belongs to Him. Each change has brought new life to what we were doing on His behalf.

How about you? Have you gotten into a rut in your Christian life? If so, God has been waiting for you to be willing to change. Why not pray right now for God to steer you back on course to a higher place . . . beyond belief?

LOVE

"Love is patient, love is kind. It does not envy, it does not boast, it is not proud. It is not rude, it is not self-seeking, it is not easily angered, it keeps no record of wrongs. Love does not delight in evil but rejoices with the truth. It always protects, always trusts, always hopes, always perseveres. Love never fails."

1 Corinthians 13:4-8

Love
Words and music by Bob Hartman
© 1990 by Petsong Publishing/SESAC.
All rights reserved. Used by permission.

Love is patient, love is kind,
no eyes of envy, true love is blind.
Love is humble, it knows no pride,
no selfish motive hidden inside.
Love is gentle, makes no demands,
despite all wrong, true love still stands.
Love is holy, love is pure,
it lasts forever, it will endure.

Chorus
Love knows when to let go,
love knows when to say "No."
Love grows in the light of the Son
and love shows the world that
the Son of Love has come.

Love is loyal, believes the best. It loves
the truth, love stands the test.
Love is God sent in His Son,
love forgives all we have done.

Repeat chorus

In this world where hatred seems to
grow, true love goes against the flow
and becomes so hard to show. In this
world where push turns into shove, we
have strength to rise above through the
power of His love. Lord, we need to
know the power of Your love.

Repeat chorus

While channel surfing on the radio, we may hear the Foreigner song "I Want to Know What Love Is." We live in a world that desperately wants to know what true love is. Unfortunately, most of the time we are "looking in all the wrong places." Our idea of love is often defined by what we see in films, music and literature.

In 1 Corinthians 13, often called the Love Chapter, we read God's definition. God knows a lot about love. He originated love. He *is* love! (1 John 4:8). Memorize 1 Corinthians 13! We need a constant reminder of what true godly love is. We need to use this as the litmus test in all of our relationships.

A line in the chorus of this song says, "Love knows when to say 'No.'" I know this as a father. It is so hard to tell someone we love, "No." But that is often the most loving answer we can give because love "always protects." Some of you reading this may be at odds with your parents over what you can and can't do. Sometimes it's very hard for us to see the same dangers our parents can see. When they tell us "No," we are often resentful, but as we can see in this Scripture, they are exercising true love. I also know as a parent how easy it is to *not* live up to these verses, but it is my goal to get closer and closer.

Read this Scripture slowly and thoughtfully, thinking about each aspect. Then ask yourself how your love for your parents, husband or wife, boyfriend or girlfriend, relative and neighbor stacks up. It is only His love working through us that allows us to love as we should!

SEEN AND NOT HEARD

"Live such good lives among the pagans that, though they accuse you of doing wrong, they may see your good deeds and glorify God on the day he visits us."

1 Peter 2:12

Seen and Not Heard
Words and music by Bob Hartman
© 1990 by Petsong Publishing/SESAC.
All rights reserved. Used by permission.

Too many black sheep in the family,
too many stones from a house of glass.
They've heard the story, they've
heard the lines, but talk is
too cheap to change their minds.
They want to see some vital signs.
Conviction—in the way we live,
conviction—not a narrative.
Actions speak a little louder than words.

Chorus
Seen and not heard, seen and not heard,
sometimes God's children
should be seen and not heard.
Seen and not heard, seen and not heard,
sometimes God's children
should be seen and not heard.
There's too much talk and not enough
walk. Sometimes God's children
should be seen and not heard.

Delayed reaction to hostility brings us
into reality 'cause when we answer in
our defense they can see
through the false pretense.
They want to see some evidence.
Commitment—no more alibis,
commitment—not a compromise.
Actions speak a little louder than words.

Repeat chorus

Let your light so shine in all you do
with an answer near when they come to
you. Don't let your mouth start talkin'
until your feet start walkin'.

Repeat chorus

I wrote this song during one of the darkest times for Christians I have seen in my lifetime, a time when television news programs featured stories of high-profile televangelists who were not practicing what they preached. I was embarrassed for God, just as you may have been. I was also tired of seeing Christians portrayed in the media as hypocrites and con artists.

I became thoroughly convinced that our testimony to the world is not so much in what we say but how we live. People don't need any more of our lofty rhetoric; they need to see action which speaks louder than words. They need to see Christ lived out in our lives on and off TV, on and off the stage, and in and out of church. They can argue about the existence of God or about our moral convictions but it's hard to argue about a life that has been changed by the power of God. 1 Peter 2:12 makes it evident that even though they may falsely accuse us, they can still see our good works.

Some of the hardest people to witness to are the members of our own family because they know us so well. I recall many failed attempts myself as a young Christian. It took many years of watching my life for some of them to come around. I guess I finally realized I could preach more sermons with my life than I could with my mouth! I started to show them instead of tell them.

Why not try to show someone Christ in your life today—possibly through an act of kindness, compassion or concern? I'm sure you will see a difference in their response.

PRAYER

"Pray continually."
1 Thessalonians 5:17

First I want to thank You, Lord, for
being who You are, for coming to the
rescue of a man who's drifted far,
for calling me to be Your son and calling
me to serve—Lord, the way You've
blessed my life is more than I deserve.
Keep the ones I love so dearly,
fill their emptiness while I am gone,
and fill the loneliness in me.

Chorus
This is my prayer lifted to You,
knowing You care even more than I do.
This is my prayer lifted in Your name.
Your will be done I humbly pray.

Let me be the evidence of what Your
grace can do to a generation
struggling to find themselves in You.
May they come to know the love of God,
may their eyes be made to see.
Give me the opportunity to share the
truth that sets them free.
And may unity in all things be the banner
of Your church, and let revival's fire
begin to burn, begin to burn.

Repeat chorus

As we face the last and final hours, turn
a wayward country back to You. And
keep us from the evil that devours, keep
us on the path and lead us through. Keep
us in Your light until Your kingdom
comes and our work is done.

This is my prayer lifted to You, knowing
You care even more than I do. This is my
prayer in Jesus' name. Your will be done
I humbly pray, this is my prayer.

We had just begun work on *Beyond Belief* when we realized we needed another song. John and Dino Elefante and I were sitting around discussing what kind of a song it should be. They said, "Bob, we wish that you would write something very personal." John had a great melody idea which he put down on cassette with what we call a "scat" vocal idea, which amounts to not much more than mouthing syllables. I'm sure John would have been embarrassed to let someone else hear it, but the emotion of the song was there. I took the tape to my hotel room and wrote the lyrics in about a day.

It actually was an easier song to write than most because it is definitely Petra's prayer. It begins with thanksgiving for all God has done—our salvation, His calling and His many blessings. Next we pray for the families who count the days until we're home again. Many people who travel in their jobs have written to tell us how meaningful that was to them. We then pray for our ministry to reach many people, much like the prayer we pray every night before taking the stage, and for the Church, the body of all believers, to be strong, united and to experience revival. As Jesus taught His disciples to pray in the Lord's Prayer, we pray for God to keep us from evil until the end of the age.

It is always a very special time for us when we perform this song. We literally pray as we sing. Thanks to all of you who have heard and agreed with us in our "Prayer."

Thanksgiving should always be a regular part of our prayers—not just in the month of November—but always!

One of my special memories took place when we were traveling with Josh McDowell during the *Why Wait?* tour. On one particular night, our performance was not up to par, and, I was very disappointed with my part. When the altar call was given, I didn't really expect much of a response, despite the fact that there were over 6,000 people in attendance. To my surprise, every aisle was packed.

We had to ask three times for more counselors to help minister. The sight of all those people filling up the aisles and stairs—giving their hearts and lives to Jesus Christ—was something I'll never forget ... ever. Once again, the Lord reminded me that it is by His Spirit that people are drawn to Jesus and hearts are changed. It's certainly not by any work we do.
—John Schlitt

33

1989   1992

DESTINY

*"'For I know the plans I have for you,' declares the
LORD, 'plans to prosper you and not to harm you,
plans to give you hope and a future.'" Jeremiah 29:11*

Destiny

Words by Bob Hartman
Music by John Elefante
© 1991 by Petsong Publishing (admin. by Word,
Inc.)/SESAC and Uncle Pitts Publishing/BMI.
All rights reserved. Used by permission.

Time is a gift on loan, fate is already
known. It's your destiny to make it to
the end, it's your destiny to go against
the trend, heavenly destiny, destiny.

Plans are already laid, debts are already
paid (paid in full). It's your destiny,
your place within His will,
it's your destiny, you alone can fill,
heavenly destiny, destiny.

When you gonna see you're meant to
be, you're chosen out of history?
No one else can take your place,
the one and only in the human race—one
of a kind. When you gonna see He has a
will for you and only you?
Fulfill your destiny.

The steps of a righteous man are led by a
Master's plan. It's your destiny, don't
forsake the call. It's your destiny, a stone
within the wall. It's your destiny, no
accidental call. It's your destiny, you
were meant to be. It's your destiny, only
you can see, heavenly destiny, destiny.

I can clearly remember the feelings I
had when I first left my small Ohio town
to go to college. The three-and-a-half-
hour trip was usually made at night and
it was often a time of deep reflection. I
remember looking up into the stars and
feeling so small and insignificant. I
didn't know who I was or where I was
going. I didn't know what this world
was about. I didn't know Christ. A couple of years later, I met the One who had
all of those answers. I met Jesus Christ.
I met the One who knew all about me,
and yet loved me enough to come into
my life!

I won't forget the feeling I had when I
realized that God had plans for *me!* This
fact became such an anchor to my life. It

meant that God knew where I fit into this world and what I was meant to do. It meant that I had a purpose, a destiny!

From this Scripture, we can see what God's plans for us are about. He wants us to prosper. He wants to give us hope and a future! His intentions are all for our good. And we can be confident that "he who began a good work in you will carry it on to completion until the day of Christ Jesus" (Philippians 1:6). Now, we can face each day with confidence, knowing God is accomplishing His plans in our lives when we yield to Him. Just knowing that He has good plans for us helps us through times we don't understand. It helps us to know that there is a reason for our existence and a purpose that only we can fulfill.

Have you ever felt that your life had no purpose? I encourage you to read Jeremiah 29:11 carefully and make it your own. It will help you to see that you have a heavenly destiny!

SIGHT UNSEEN

"Then Jesus told him, 'Because you have seen me, you have believed; blessed are those who have not seen and yet have believed.'"   *John 20:29*

Sight Unseen

Words and music by Bob Hartman
© 1991 by Petsong Publishing
(admin. by Word, Inc.)/SESAC.
All rights reserved. Used by permission.

For so long I was depending upon my
senses and fences, I tried to ride on.
And trusting in things that can never be
seen was always a crutch on which
others must lean. Thinking if I could
see I would believe, then somebody
said believe and you will see.

Chorus
Sight unseen, sight unseen,
you have to take it sight unseen.
Sight unseen, sight unseen,
you have to take it sight unseen.
Blinded by the darkness only
faith can come between
sight unseen, sight unseen.

Evidence built into every design led to
conviction between every line.
Faith is the key that can open the veil
to love incarnated and pierced with a
nail. Listen, my friends, have I got
news for you: The nails in His
hands and feet were meant for you.

Repeat chorus

Every person has faith in something—such as faith that when we flip a light switch, the light will come on; or faith that the law of gravity will keep us from floating away. Electricity and gravity are things that we cannot see. In this Scripture and in this song, we are told that we will be blessed for believing in our Lord, whom we have not seen. The Christian walk is a walk of faith—faith in what we have not seen. In fact, a scriptural definition of faith is provided in Hebrews 11:1: "Now faith is being sure of what we hope for and certain of what we do not see."

In many ways, it would seem easier to follow Christ if faith wasn't involved. He could just speak to us audibly or send

us a fax about decisions we should make. If
either one of these ever happened to me, I
would have no trouble following! But it
wouldn't be faith. And we are told in
Hebrews 11:6 that only faith pleases Him.

He doesn't want us to just live by a set of
ethical rules. He wants us to have an intimate
daily communion with Him, to the end that
we might *know* Him! He is the focus and the
object of our faith. The things that we see
often confuse and perplex us. They are the
things that cannot always be trusted, the
things that are temporal and not eternal. God
wants us to use our spiritual eyes to "see"
that which comes after believing.

*To those who would say, "I'll believe it when I see
it," we should reply, "You'll see it when you believe
it." There is no other way to come to God. It is
always a leap of faith. We always have to take it
"sight unseen."*

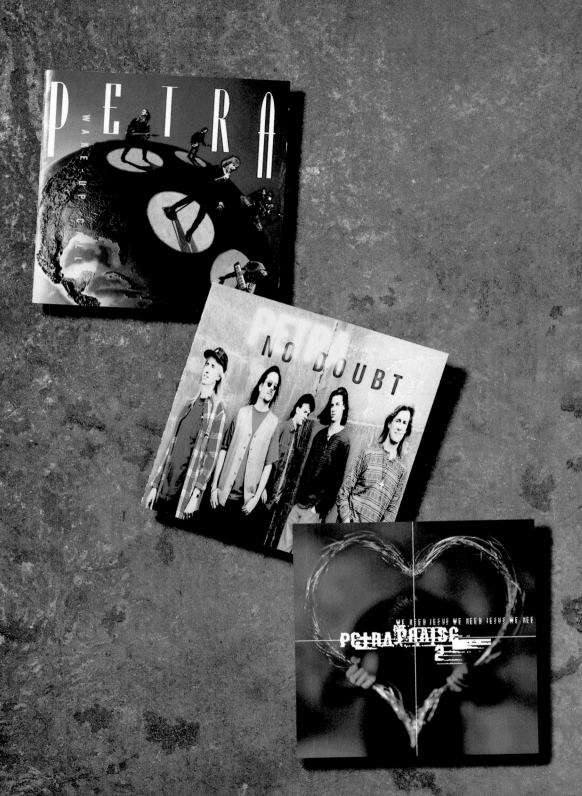

Wake-Up Call (1993)

Song List

Midnight Oil
Good News
Strong Convictions
He's Been in My Shoes
Praying Man
Underneath the Blood
Sleeping Giant
Believer in Deed
Marks of the Cross
Just Reach Out

The desire for change and the need to work at home in a studio in Nashville instead of California, where John and Dino resided, led us to Brown Bannister as producer. It was a risk on our part, because Brown was not known as a rock producer and had not worked with many bands. We were late getting started and had firm deadlines to meet, which resulted in a rushed project again. *Wake-Up Call* had many great moments, but what we hoped would be the end in our search for change became just another step in the process.

No Doubt (1995)

Song List

With John and Dino Elefante relocating to Nashville and building a world-class studio, it was a natural choice to work with them again. The time away from one another was very healthy for both us and John and Dino. As a result, we were able to approach the recording process in a whole new way. Changes often come hard and there were certainly moments of agony, but we believe the result was something very different for us. Although I feel the changing is not over, I believe we are much closer to where we need to be.

Only time will tell the success of this record, but the initial response has been great. Both the title song and "Right Place" have been successful on radio— and we have high hopes for continued success both in concert, and in the popularity of the record.

The lyrics are intended to strengthen and uplift, and the music can be characterized as more rhythmic than previous albums. Upon completion of the record, I felt the Lord leading me to no longer tour with the band full-time. Rather, I would devote my entire energy to the recordings of the group. After 23 years, this was a big change, but one I know the Lord directed. It is our hope and prayer that this transition will result in a more effective ministry. The production quality is the best ever and the band has a new life and energy from stage. We all remain thankful to God for allowing us to do what we love for Him.

Petra Praise II: We Need Jesus (1997)

Song List

Lord, I Lift Your
Name on High

Song of Moses/
Revelation 15:3, 4

Be of Good Cheer

Show Your Power

I Love You, Lord

The Holiest Name

Let Our Voices
Rise Like Incense

Ancient of Days

I Waited

Lovely Lord

Medley: Only by
Grace/ To Him Who
Sits on the Throne/
You Are Holy

We Need Jesus

Ever since we released our first praise record, we have looked for the right time to record a sequel. This time around, we were able to spend more time planning and I really like the selection of songs we were able to adapt to a "Petra" style. This album includes four original songs as well as a cover of John and Dino's "We Need Jesus." We chose this as the subtitle because it sums up so many things. It is the continuing message of the ministry of Petra, and the recognition that we need Him keeps us praising Him for His goodness. Praise has always been an important part of Petra's concerts and there will certainly be some new additions from this recording.

We were thrilled that Lou Gramm joined John Schlitt and John Elefante on the vocals for the title song. Just think, the former lead singer of Head East (Schlitt), the former singer of Kansas (Elefante) and the singer of Foreigner, joining together to sing, "We Need Jesus!" God is so good! We pray that this album touches many lives.

PRAYING MAN

"The prayer of a righteous man is powerful and effective."   *James 5:16*

Praying Man

Words by John Lawry
Music by John Lawry and Jim Cooper
© 1993 by Stop Shakin' Pub. and Jimmy Vision
Music/BMI. All rights reserved. International
copyright secured. Used by permission.

Noah saw the coming of the flood—
he built an ark upon dry land.
When Moses prayed, God parted the
Red Sea—in faith he made his stand.
And David dropped the giant to his
knees—empowered by a stronger hand.
God changed the course of history—see
the power of the praying man.

Chorus
Faith lives in folded hands, mountains
move when you make a stand.
It's never been a case of sleight of hand,
it's the power, oh, the power of the
praying man. Whoa, I see the power of
the praying man, whoa, I see the
power of the praying man.

Jesus turned the water into wine—
no tricks, no magician.
He rules the earth, the wind, the sky—
in control of the situation.
He knew that . . .

Chorus

Prayer is alive and well today—
it's a matter of dedication.
Prayer works when you take the time to
pray—it's a matter of true devotion.
You'll see that . . .

Repeat chorus

Prayer works! "Praying Man," written by John Lawry and Jim Cooper, gives us a biblical overview of how ordinary people like you and me were used by God in powerful ways because they prayed. The title in no way means to exclude women; in fact, some of the most powerful prayer warriors in our churches today are women. It is still a mystery to me how the course of history can be changed when people pray, but thank God, I don't have to figure it out to know that it does.

The song points to several examples from the Bible, but I know firsthand how prayer has affected the ministry of Petra. There have been many faithful people who have prayed for our ministry over the years, and we have certainly seen the effects of their prayers. So many doors have opened to us for no apparent reason other than people were praying.

I remember vividly how we prayed that we might join forces with a Christian speaker, someone who was well respected and well known to the church. Someone like . . . Josh McDowell. It wasn't much more than a year later that we were on tour with Josh and his "Why Wait?" campaign. We know that God did that. And we also know why. There were thousands and thousands of young people touched through that tour and I will always cherish that experience.

Great things happen when we get alone with God. We receive direction. We intercede for others. And we get to know Him better, as we spend time praising Him!

When we pray according to God's will and in the name of Jesus Christ, powerful and exciting things happen. I hope that you are a part of a fellowship of believers with whom you pray regularly. You, too, will experience the power of a praying man.

UNDERNEATH THE BLOOD

"How much more, then, will the blood of Christ, who through the eternal Spirit offered himself unblemished to God, cleanse our consciences from acts that lead to death, so that we may serve the living God!"
Hebrews 9:14

Underneath the Blood
Words by Bob Hartman
Music by Ronny Cates
© 1993 by Petsong Pub. (admin. by Word, Inc.)/SESAC and Rowdy's Groove Music/BMI. All rights reserved. International copyright secured. Used by permission.

I was just a young man with a burning fuse, headed in the wrong way 'til I heard the news 'bout a substitution, blood shed for me, 'bout a grace so amazing it can make a man free. Now I'm rescued, pulled from the mud, it's all behind me, under the blood.

Chorus
Underneath the blood,
through the cleansing flood.
Guilt is left behind,
never brought to mind.
I'm an innocent man
underneath the blood.

Now a little older, I recall the past, farther from me than east is from west. But in all the wisdom that my growing brings I can't seem to put down all my childish things. Where do I go when I've missed the mark and my heart starts feeling like it's stained and dark? Only know one way to go— I take it to the crimson flow.

Repeat chorus

Underneath the blood,
pulled up from the mud,
feet on solid ground,
what was lost is found.
I'm an innocent man
underneath the blood.

I don't know why God chose the shedding of blood to be essential to man's forgiveness but I know that without it, there *is* no forgiveness (Hebrews 9:22). It began with the first covenant between God and man. The priests would sprinkle blood on the tabernacle and everything used in its ceremony (Hebrews 9:21). Everything under this blood was then clean, but this was not the "real thing." As with many parts of the first covenant, it was merely a foreshadowing of what was to follow. The earthly tabernacle was just a representation of the real tabernacle in Heaven.

In the New Covenant, Jesus Christ Himself, our High Priest, presented His own blood in the heavenly tabernacle. This fulfilled the requirement or payment of blood forever. There would never need to be another animal sacrifice because Christ's blood was the "real thing." But His blood didn't just cover over sin; He removed it.

By claiming Christ's sacrifice for me personally, I am underneath the blood and my sin has been removed "as far as the east is from the west" (Psalm 103:12). God sees me through the veil of Christ's blood; therefore I am perfect in His eyes. Of course, I still constantly need His forgiveness. I sin every day, sometimes without knowing it. But we have the promise that "if we confess our sins, he is faithful and just and will forgive us our sins and purify us from all unrighteousness" (1 John 1:9). In this way, we can abide underneath His blood.

What do you need to confess to Him today? Take it to Him and leave it there, knowing that He is more than able to forgive and give you a brand-new start. Praise Him for the power available in His blood.

BELIEVER IN DEED

"Dear children, let us not love with words or tongue but with actions and in truth." **I John 3:18**

Believer in Deed

On this journey we begin at birth, this
fleeting moment that we spend on earth,
no second chance to live it all again—
it must be now or never to cherish
each endeavor. What will they say
that I have left behind? A faithful
heritage for all to find. What will
they see? I want my legacy to be . . .

Chorus
He was a believer in deed,
he had a heart of a different breed.
He made his mark and he lived by his
creed, a true believer, a believer in deed.

Am I living everything I say?
Am I pointing others to the way?
Will I leave this world a better place?
Will Jesus say He knew me?
Is Jesus living through me?
Did I maintain my authenticity?
A man of honor and integrity?
Remembering me I hope that
they will truly see . . .

Repeat chorus

At the end of my days I know I'm gonna
say I wouldn't live my life any other
way. I'll look to my posterity to carry on
for me, and pray that they will see . . .

Repeat chorus

This song expresses my desire to be thought of as someone who lives out his faith daily. It is very personal. I remember thinking of my son as I was writing it. He is now eight years old and I pray that when he is older and I am no longer here, he will think of me as a man who truly believed what he said and lived what he believed. In order for that to be the case I must live consistently today, tomorrow and the next day, teaching him about the things of God by example.

It is amazing that even at his young age he is very perceptive of any inconsistencies in my attitude, reactions and behavior. In fact, no one else except my wife will be in a better position to judge my life. From me, he learns who God is and what He is like. He learns what loving and following God means. He learns how a man should treat his wife, loving her as Christ loved the church. He learns how a man should treat others with dignity and respect. It is an awesome responsibility to be a father and an even more awesome responsibility to be a consistent Christian.

In my travels with Petra around the world, I am constantly reminded that we are being observed both on and off the stage. Because we deliberately and unashamedly identify with Christ, we are representatives of Him wherever we go and whatever we do. Whether in an airport or a truck stop, a church or a nightclub, we are being watched. In every action and every reaction we are representing our Lord in a positive or a negative way. I can only hope as others have looked at my life, they could say, "He is a believer in deed."

Who is watching you to see if your attitudes and actions are consistent with your beliefs? Ask the Father to help you as you strive to be the best example for Him you can possibly be.

MARKS OF THE CROSS

"' By this all men will know that you are my disciples, if you love one another.'"   *John 13:35*

Marks of the Cross

These days shallow and feeble resolve abound, and true devotion and passionate fervor are seldom found. But there are those who often feel they're all alone, those whose identities are known by the mark of the crucified Son.

Chorus
Praying, caring, loving, sharing— these are the marks of the cross. Giving, bearing, feeling, daring to lay down your life on the line, forgetting what you leave behind, and willing to suffer the loss of the marks of the cross.

These days the search for detachment and solitude lead to retreating to fortresses no one would dare intrude. Then there are those whose restless burdens start to show, those who unmistakably must know there's no crown 'til we suffer the cross.

Repeat chorus

All our identity rests in the knowledge of who we're created to be. We are His workmanship made in His image for all of creation to see the marks of His pain and His glory.

Repeat chorus

Jesus tells His disciples that the greatest evidence that they belong to Him is the love that they have for each other. I believe that Satan knows this as well, and this is why he is hard at work in our churches and fellowships to bring division and disunity. He knows that if we truly followed the words of Christ, the world would beat a path to our door. The kind of love He spoke of is rare and unique and, most of all, godly.

In the previous verse, Jesus said that we should love each other the way He loves us. His is the most self-sacrificing love the world has ever seen. We can only do this through Christ Himself. Once we recognize how we are unconditionally loved by God, we can begin to allow that love to overflow to others.

"Marks of the Cross" talks about many practical ways in which that love is manifested. Praying, caring, sharing, giving, bearing, feeling and daring to lay down our lives on the line: these are the "marks" of the cross of Christ in our lives. The most important attribute of this love is its sacrificial nature. We sacrifice our time, our money, our own needs and whatever else keeps us from putting others before ourselves. This kind of love that "all men will know" comes only from God, and it attracts like a magnet! It makes people want what we've got.

If you want to have this kind of love for others, you need only draw closer to Christ and discover more about how He loves you. As you do, I am confident He will present you with opportunities that will allow that love to flow to others. Then you too will have the marks of the cross in your life.

JUST REACH OUT

"The Spirit of the Sovereign LORD *is on me, because the* LORD *has anointed me to preach good news to the poor. He has sent me to bind up the brokenhearted, to proclaim freedom for the captives and release from darkness for the prisoners."* Isaiah 61:1

Just Reach Out

Sometimes the night seems to go on for
days when it's hard to see the light
through the darkness and haze.
While the world around you makes you
feel out of place and the burdens that
you carry are just too hard to face.

Chorus
Just reach out and He'll reach in,
take your broken heart and make it
whole again. It don't matter who
you are or where you've been,
just reach out and He'll reach in.

Standing in a crowd but still all alone,
crying out for answers that nobody
knows. Everybody's busy looking out
for themselves. Is there anyone who
really cares about anyone else?

Repeat chorus

You say you've walked ten thousand
steps away but don't you know
that it's only one step back?
Because the One who hears you when
you pray is the One who's there beside
you—and He'll never walk away.

Repeat chorus

Songwriters John Schlitt and Rich
Gootee vividly convey the picture of
God reaching out to us in "Just Reach
Out." We have a God who longs to
reach into our lives and heal us.
Knowing Christ does not insulate us
from having a broken heart. Many times
in our lives, people let us down. We feel
disappointed, lonely and hurt. But
Christ Himself faced these same feelings
while here on earth, so we can truly say,
"He knows just how you feel."

The healing process takes our faith. In
James 4:8 we have the promise that if
we draw near to God, He will come near
to us. It is an act of our faith to reach out
to God in our times of need. And when

we do, we have the promise from Psalm 34:17 that "the righteous cry out, and the LORD hears them; he delivers them from all their troubles."

It is the human tendency to reach out to everyone else first. We look to other people to fill our need, but we are often left in a worse condition than when we started. Why not reach out to Him first and go directly to the only source of true inner healing? I have noticed many times that the Lord will bring someone for me to minister to when I am feeling sorry for myself. I think this happens so that we can tell them what we ourselves need to hear. After I give of myself during my own time of need, I feel the touch of God in my own life. Afterward, it is always remarkable how small my problems seem and how sufficient God is.

The next time you feel this way, try reaching out to God first, and then look for someone else to minister to. You will be amazed at the results!

ENTER IN

"Therefore, brothers, since we have confidence to enter the Most Holy Place by the blood of Jesus, by a new and living way opened for us through the curtain, that is, his body." — Hebrews 10:19, 20

Enter In

Words by Bob Hartman. Music by Jim Cooper and John Elefante. © 1995 Petsong Pub. (admin. by Word, Inc.)/SESAC/Jimmy Vision Music/Uncle Pitts Music/BMI. All rights reserved. International copyright secured. Used by permission.

Once a year for sacrifice just one priest could pay the price and step inside the inner veil to make the people free. Temple stood the same for years till the Nazarene appears, things will never be the same since 33 A.D. When He spoke and bowed His head, He who saved the world was dead. Then the earth began to shake, Heaven's wall began to break, opening the Holy Place, the temple veil is torn in two, the way is clear for me and you.

Chorus
We can enter in, enter in, into Heaven's Holy Place. We can enter in, enter in, boldly by His blood we can approach His throne of grace. We can enter in a new and living way, by our faith He will receive us when we pray.

Now without a second look we forget what all it took to be seen as innocent by His holy eyes. Never thinking foolishly, there is something He won't see, for our lack of righteousness there is no disguise. He won't look the other way, someone's life will have to pay, once for all it has been done, taken out upon His Son. He remembers it no more, now for us He is the Door opened up forevermore.

Repeat chorus

We can enter in, enter in, we can enter in His gates with thankfulness and praise. We can enter in, enter in into this once forbidden Holy Place. We can enter in, enter in, we can live in goodness and in mercy all our days.

In this song, I wanted to describe the monumental change that took place the day of crucifixion. No longer could only one priest enter into the Holy of Holies. The way was made for every believer to enter into the real Holy of Holies not made by hands.

The marvel is that through our belief in Christ, we can come boldly into the very presence of God. It is easy to take for granted what a miracle and a privilege this is! If you are at all like me, you end up praying in the midst of other activities. While driving, it's, "Lord, don't let me have a wreck!" While taking a test, it might be, "Lord, help me remember!" But seldom do we consider what is happening in Heaven when we

pray. We can enter into His presence any-
time we want. We are clothed in the very
righteousness of Christ Himself so we can
boldly come before Him. We have access in
"a new and living way" made possible by the
blood of our Lord Jesus Christ.

The moment Christ gave up His spirit, the
huge veil in the temple that separated man
from the Holy of Holies, the most Holy
Place, was torn from top to bottom
(Matthew 27:51). This veil was about 60 feet
high and thickly woven. No human hands
could have torn it. Only God could have, and
by this gesture, we can assume that God
meant business! How can we ever take prayer
for granted after knowing the extent of
God's miracle on our behalf?

*The next time you pray, try picturing yourself as
God does: clothed in the righteousness of His Son and
standing in His presence. I guarantee your prayers
will take on a new reverence and a new meaning.
Things have truly never been the same since A.D. 33!*

THINK TWICE

"Flee the evil desires of youth, and pursue righteousness, faith, love and peace, along with those who call on the Lord out of a pure heart." **2 Timothy 2:22**

Think Twice

Words by Bob Hartman. Music by John Elefante,
Ronny Cates and Jim Cooper
© 1995 Petsong Pub. (admin. by Word,
Inc.)/SESAC/Uncle Pitts Music/Rowdy's Groove
Music/Jimmy Vision Music/BMI. All rights reserved.
International copyright secured. Used by permission.

You could think of times when you had
the right chance, you could make a
choice when nobody could see.
You could think of ways of
defending your deeds, justify
the way that you wanted to be.
Wait, just a minute.
Wait, just a minute.

Chorus
Hey, did you ever think twice?
Something inside says, "Stay away."
Hey, did you ever think twice?
When there's still time you can go the
other way. Hey, did you ever think
twice? If you don't bother, gonna pay
the price. Hey, did you ever think twice?

You could think of things that you
wanted to try, you could think of things
that you wish you could see. You could
go a way that would seem so right,
thinking of a place that you wish you
could be. Wait, just a minute.
Wait, just a minute.

Repeat chorus

Face to face with sin—you better
think again, you better think again.
Take another look for a second time
and give a second thought to
where you draw the line.
Wait, just a minute.
Wait, just a minute.

Repeat chorus

There is that moment of time for each of us, when faced with temptation, that we contemplate whether or not to sin. This song challenges us to "think twice," to realize the ramifications of our choices. Instead of rushing into sin, we should "wait just a minute" and take time to think it through. Do we really want to hurt God, ourselves and others or do we want to honor God with our lives by making the right choices?

Although I have made many wrong choices in my life, I can point to a few choices that were right, such as the choice I made to go to Bible college instead of taking a very good job. I knew that the Lord was calling me to go to Bible college, and I wanted to follow Him, so that choice was very clear. But I didn't see 23 years of ministry with Petra that came as a result of that choice. You see, Petra was formed at that Bible college.

What may seem like little things at the time can impact our whole lives. Unfortunately, this can work in negative ways as well. One mistake that we think at the time is no big deal can cost us dearly the rest of our lives.

In this Scripture, we are told to flee the evil desires of youth. We should run the other way much as Joseph did when confronted with the temptation of adultery. He "thought twice" about the consequences. First, he would be sinning against his God, whom he loved. Secondly, he would be betraying the trust of Potiphar, her husband and his employer. Whatever he was thinking, it made him leave his robe and run as fast as he could in the opposite direction! Making the right choices is what life is really about.

Why can't we be just as wise as Joseph? We can. We can "wait just a minute" and take time to "think twice," while there's still time to "go the other way"!

HEART OF A HERO

"Be strong and take heart, all you who hope in the LORD.*"*   *Psalm 31:24*

Heart of a Hero
Words by Brian Wooten
Music by Jim Cooper and Brian Wooten
© 1995 No Choice Pub./Jimmy Vision Music/BMI.
All rights reserved. International copyright
secured. Used by permission.

The fearless giant faced a brave young
shepherd boy. He said, "Your God is
dead and your nation soon destroyed."
But the son of Jesse proved what
God can do in the heart of a hero.

Three men refused to bow to the idol
made of gold. They knew they could
burn for not doing what they're told.
They'd rather face the fire than
to kneel to a god made by hands.

Chorus
It takes the heart of a hero
to stand for what's right.
It takes the heart of a hero
to lay down your life.

There are idols to be worshiped and
giants in the land. They'll drag you
down, attack your faith and slay you if
they can. So let your heart be filled with
courage and strength of the Lord.

Repeat chorus

Have the faith of a child and the power
of God, and when you call on His name,
He will give you the heart of a hero.

Will you stand for what's right?
Would you lay down your life?
Do you have the heart?

Repeat chorus

Using biblical examples, this song teaches that it takes real heart and courage to make a stand for God. It may really cost us to make that stand. We may lose friends, popularity or even our lives, but we know we are in good company with many believers throughout the centuries who have taken a stand for God and kept the faith.

Shortly after becoming a Christian, I was taking a psychology course. One day, the professor made a statement that contradicted the biblical view of man. A young man promptly raised his hand, disagreed with the professor and proceeded to give the Christian view in front of the whole class. This took great courage. We are conditioned to think of college professors as infallible. There may have been no one else but me who agreed with him, and I deeply regret my silence to this day.

What admiration I had for that "hero" who took a stand for his faith without concern for its popularity! I am thankful for this student's example of courage. If for no other reason, I believe God wanted me to see what it means to stand for one's faith. Since those days as a young Christian, I have had many opportunities to take a stand for my faith. It demands laying down your life to the point of disregarding your own reputation, and it takes an absolute conviction of God's truth. It takes the heart of a hero.

Every day God gives us opportunities to allow His power to flow through us. Sometimes we miss them because we are too concerned about what others might think. Remember this: God didn't call us to be popular; He called us to be faithful. Will you have the heart of a hero today?

MORE THAN A THOUSAND WORDS

*"In the same way, the Spirit helps us in our weakness.
We do not know what we ought to pray for, but the
Spirit himself intercedes for us with groans that words
cannot express."*　　　　　　　　　　　　*Romans 8:26*

More Than a Thousand Words

I saw Your picture hanging on the wall—
just an artist rendering, that was all.
The way You looked down in Your
agony jogged my memory and helped
me to see if a picture's worth a thousand
words, then it won't help me at all.
Only words are never gonna say
what I feel for You today.

Chorus
More than a thousand words won't say
more than my life will not repay.
More than a thousand things I do
won't make it up to You.

I stopped a moment sitting all alone
without a waiting call on the phone.
Looked like a picture from a magazine,
more serenity than I've ever seen.
And if words cannot describe this day
or the beauty of this scene,
tell me, how can I expect the words
I say to reflect the things I mean?

Repeat chorus

More than a thousand words won't tell
how You forgave me when I fell.
More than a thousand words
won't do to say, "I love You."

Simple words will never quite
express my gratitude to You.
Until I cross the barrier,
mortal words will have to do.

Repeat chorus

Sometimes there just aren't words to describe how we feel about God, those heartfelt times when we experience the awe of being redeemed. We could not begin to describe the feeling even if we used a "thousand words." It's frustrating when we can't put our feelings into words, but we can rest assured that the Spirit is helping us in those times.

The second verse of this song describes a quiet time alone with God, reflecting on His beautiful work of nature. In today's busy world, we must make a special effort to find these times. We need to get away from the phone, the TV, friends and family and just be alone with God. In these times, I hear God's voice in my heart the clearest.

In Luke 10:38-42, we read the story of Mary and Martha. Martha was busy preparing the meal, but Mary simply sat at the feet of Jesus and listened to Him. When Martha complained to the Lord, He didn't agree with her; He told her she was worried and upset about many things, but Mary had chosen what was better.

So often, I am more like Martha than Mary. I am worried and upset about many things and I don't take the time to be alone with Jesus and just listen. When I finally *do* take the time, I am amazed at how small my worries become and how great the Lord becomes. It is His greatness that becomes so difficult to put into words, but He surely doesn't mind us trying!

Why not find the time today to just be alone with God? Clear your mind of everything else and just tell Him how great He is. You will be amazed at how different you feel.

NO DOUBT

"But when he asks, he must believe and not doubt, because he who doubts is like a wave of the sea, blown and tossed by the wind."   *James 1:6*

No Doubt

Words by Bob Hartman
Music by John Elefante and Ronny Cates
© 1995 Petsong Pub. (admin. by Word,
Inc.)/SESAC/Uncle Pitts Music/Rowdy's Groove
Music/BMI. All rights reserved. International
copyright secured. Used by permission.

There are times when you feel like you can't go on, there are times when you feel like giving in. And there are times when you feel like you can't try anymore, there are times of trouble in believing. This test of your faith will last as long as it takes to pass till you have no more doubt you'll endure and your faith will emerge true and pure.

Chorus
No doubt it'll be all right, with God it'll all work together for good. No doubt in the end it will be understood. No doubt it'll all work out, with faith He can move any mountain for us—no doubt in the power of Jesus. And after all is done, we find out all we really need to have is no doubt.

There's a time to take a reckless leap of faith, there's a time to be cautious and wait. And there's a way of learning from the past that this time of trouble won't last. And sometimes we want to think we know the ways He will choose to make us grow. But it's never the way of our choosing and we can't always see what He's using.

Repeat chorus

There will be winters in the seasons of our soul with a cold and bitter wind that chills our lives. But our faith can be building a fire that will warm us till springtime arrives.

Part of the Christian life is going through times of discouragement and things that we just don't understand. Have you ever felt like a wave of the sea, blown and tossed by the wind? I have. It is only our faith and the grace of God that carries us through those times. But all too often, we doubt our beliefs and believe our doubts. If we heed Romans 10:17—"Consequently, faith comes from hearing the message, and the message is heard through the word of Christ"— then we know our answers will be found in God's Word.

If your faith is lacking, you need to go to God's Word to be built up again. You can start by reading some of the many promises that tell us we are totally and unconditionally accepted by Him. (Start with Psalm 103:1-5 and John 6:37.) Once you accept that fact, it's easier to believe Romans 8:28: "And we know that in all things God works for the good of those who love him, who have been called according to his purpose." Notice it says *all things!* Even things that don't appear to be good at the time can be worked together for our good by our God. God is on your side and if *He* is for you, who can be against you?

Most of the time we still don't understand the things we're going through. But if we understood everything, would there be any need to exercise our faith? God is pleased by our faith and wants us to exercise it.

Are you walking by faith, not by sight? Try facing what lies before you with the simple trust of a child. Believe the One who loves you perfectly and, most of all, have no doubt!

RIGHT PLACE

"Dear friends, do not be surprised at the painful trial you are suffering, as though something strange were happening to you. But rejoice that you participate in the sufferings of Christ, so that you may be overjoyed when his glory is revealed."   *I Peter 4:12, 13*

Right Place

Got no place to run, gotta look up to see the bottom, no visible support—no one there you can lean on. You're all on your own—you know it's sink or swim. There is no doubt about it, you have to look to Him. When you think you've had enough, no more you can do, when you feel like giving up, deadline is in view. When your time is almost gone, you haven't got a clue, now's the time to turn your face.

Chorus
You're in the right place—trusting only Him. You're in the right place—kick back and just depend. You're in the right place—to see what He can do. You're in the right place—He will come through.

When you're sinking fast—takin' water in your boat, no one to bail you out—you think it's all she wrote. The odds are against you—your chances slim to none, a hopeless situation—you got no place to run. No one has a rescue plan waiting in the wings. Now's the time to call His name, He can do all things. When your self-reliance fails, you still have a prayer, you will have to trust His grace.

Repeat chorus

When you abide, He will provide— never shorthanded. When you will pray, He'll make a way— He won't leave you stranded.

When everything seems to fail around us and the walls of our lives are caving in, we tend to believe we are somehow out of God's will or out from under His protection. In an energetic way this song says that we are exactly where God wants us. We are in the "right place."

How can this be? The Bible teaches us that God allows our faith to be tested so that we can grow to trust Him more. But waiting for His glory to be revealed can sometimes be very painful. When we ask, "Why?", James 1:2-4 answers us: "Consider it pure joy, my brothers, whenever you face trials of many kinds, because you know that the testing of your faith develops perseverance.

"Perseverance must finish its work so that you may be mature and complete, not lacking anything."

Our faith is tested so that we might develop perseverance. *Webster's* defines perseverance as "continuing to do something in spite of difficulty or opposition." What God wants us to "continue to do" is to trust Him, follow Him and serve Him. When we are able to do this, James tells us we are "mature and complete, not lacking anything."

It is God's goal in this life to make us mature Christians, and trials are a necessary part of the equation. When we realize that even trials are a part of the process, they are much easier to bear. I wish I could say it's always a joy when a trial comes along in my life, but I haven't quite reached that point. However, I do understand it better, knowing where God is going with all of it!

What is God doing to develop perseverance in you? When you don't have anywhere else to turn but to Him, you are in the "right place."

TWO ARE BETTER THAN ONE

"Two are better than one, because they have a good return for their work: If one falls down, his friend can help him up. But pity the man who falls and has no one to help him up!"   *Ecclesiastes 4:9, 10*

Two Are Better Than One

Words by Bob Hartman
Music by Ronny Cates
© 1995 Petsong Pub. (admin. by Word, Inc.)/SESAC/Rowdy's Groove Music/BMI. All rights reserved. International copyright secured. Used by permission.

You can call me up in the night.
I will pray till you win the fight—
we're more than friends.
We walk together through any weather—we sharpen each other.

Chorus
I'll be there when you call, lift you up when you fall—two are better than one. You will pray when I'm weak, help me back on my feet—two are better than one, two are better than one.

When I start to cross the line you just seem to read my mind. And then you bust me, then turn around and trust me, You come to the rescue—
I'll do the same for you.

Repeat chorus

I don't want to go solo,
it's always better with two.
I just want someone to lift me up,
to pray and help me get through.

Repeat chorus

When we have a friend that really cares about our spiritual well-being, someone who is not afraid to tell us when we're blowing it, one to whom we can confess our faults and problems, we have found something truly great. When we fall, he will pick us up and when she falls, we will do the same for her. This kind of relationship involves a lot of trust. We have to trust the other person enough to know he wouldn't use something against us that we told him in confidence. And we ourselves must be deserving of the same kind of trust. It is the kind of relationship that we need to preserve, protect and cultivate.

If you are looking for this type of relationship, there are a few questions to ask yourself concerning the other person. Do you know that he truly wants to serve the Lord no matter what the cost? Does she gossip? Is she a good example? Does he look for opportunities to lift up others around him? Is she able to confront others in a loving way with no motives other than the other person's ultimate good? Is he a man of prayer?

If you find someone with these traits, the next question to ask is this: Do *you* possess these traits? In order for the friendship to work, it must be a two-way street. Even when you think you have found someone, proceed with caution. Remember, trust is something we earn. When we have this kind of close spiritual relationship with someone, it makes it much harder to fall away, for when we fall, we have someone to pick us up.

Are you able to say "Yes" to these questions:
- *Are you a good example?*
- *Do you keep confidences?*
- *Do you lift up others around you?*
- *Do you pray for your friends?*

SINCERELY YOURS

"Love must be sincere. Hate what is evil; cling to what is good." Romans 12:9

Sincerely Yours
Words by Bob Hartman. Music by Jim Cooper, Brian Wooten and Andy Denton © 1995 Petsong Pub. (admin. by Word, Inc.)/SESAC/Jimmy Vision Music/No Choice Pub./BMI/Word Music (a div. of Word, Inc.)/ASCAP. All rights reserved. International copyright secured. Used by permission.

I've lived in my own way and found that there's a price to pay, and I felt the emptiness without Your tenderness. Now before You I confess.

Chorus
Here is all I have to give, I offer up this life I live, I am sincerely Yours. Now in all sincerity I give You all of me, I am sincerely Yours.

This prodigal is standing here now with all my senses clear. For all You gave to me, I spent it foolishly, You've been waiting patiently.

Repeat chorus

Now I feel the weight on me is lifting, You've washed away the past. And now there is a new day dawning as long as I keep holding, as long as I keep holding fast.

I am sincerely Yours, sincerely Yours.

Repeat chorus

This song speaks of giving ourselves totally over to the Lord. It is possible to go through all the outward motions without really surrendering our hearts to Him. This issue goes directly to the root of our relationship with God. He knows our hearts. And the way we begin to know our hearts is by reading His Word and having His Holy Spirit reveal things to us. The Bible is our source of "everything we need for life and godliness" (2 Peter 1:3).

During the Persian Gulf war, thousands of Iraqi soldiers surrendered to American forces. In doing so, they came out from where they were hiding into the open, gave up their weapons and were totally at the mercy of their captors. There are several comparisons we can make when a Christian totally surrenders to God.

When we surrender to our heavenly Father, we also come out into the open with Him. We realize there is no hiding from Him who sees all and knows all. We also give up our weapons—our excuses, self-pity and rationalization. They are the weapons we use to convince ourselves that it's not our fault we haven't surrendered in the past. And finally, we throw ourselves at the mercy of our captor, the One who paid the ultimate price for us, the One who loves us most. We ask Him to fill our hearts completely and change us from within. This we must do every day.

Do you want to totally surrender to God? Or is there something in your heart you are reluctant to give over to Him? Just begin by reading His Word and asking Him to change your heart. It won't be long before you'll be saying, "Lord, I am sincerely Yours."

THINK ON THESE THINGS

"Finally, brothers, whatever is true, whatever is noble, whatever is right, whatever is pure, whatever is lovely, whatever is admirable—if anything is excellent or praiseworthy—think about such things."
Philippians 4:8

Think on These Things
Words & music by Bob Hartman
© 1995 Petsong Pub. (admin. by Word, Inc.)/SESAC. All rights reserved. International copyright secured. Used by permission.

In solitary time the thoughts run through my mind, some from the very throne, some origins unknown. I know there's a danger waiting, thoughts held in captivity—the vain imaginations that long to be set free. I hold the key with thoughts of purity.

Chorus
Whatever things are pure and true, I want to think on these things, whatever things are filled with virtue, think on these things. When my mind begins to stray I want to think the other way, think on these things, think on these things.

Into the conscious flow the tributaries go, the source from which they start, abundance of the heart. My mind has a mind of its own, choosing negativity. Only the thoughts of virtue withhold the raging sea. I turn the tide by choosing to abide.

Repeat chorus

Whatever things are honest, whatever things are just, whatever things are lovely, I will put my trust in the things that never cease to keep my heart in perfect peace.

Repeat chorus

This song addresses the battle that goes on in each one of our minds. Our thought life is where many spiritual battles are either won or lost. Paul gives us a recipe for peace of mind. In our modern world, we have found many ways to fill our thoughts. As I write this, I am sitting at a computer filled with many games, with a television and a radio close by. We have so many diversions, yet our minds can only hold so much.

The danger is that we can become so preoccupied with other things, there is no more room for God. In Psalm 10:4, it is written, "In his pride the wicked does not seek him; in all his thoughts there is no room for God."

Part of Christian maturity is taking control of our minds so they don't wander wherever they want. Thinking about the things of God is often referred to in the Bible as meditation. David prayed, "May my meditation be pleasing to him, as I rejoice in the LORD" (Psalm 104:34). It is a scary thought to realize that God is listening in! We probably offend God more with our thoughts than any other behavior. We can judge our own thoughts by using Philippians 4:8 as a test.

I fail this test many times a day, but I have found a few things that help me. Reading His Word is a must, as are reading Christian books, listening to Christian music and watching Christian videos. In doing so, I am filling my mind with the right things. When I do this, my other behaviors follow suit and my mind no longer "has a mind of its own."

Speak to the Lord about your thought life. Are you thinking about what is true and right, noble and pure, lovely, admirable and praiseworthy? Ask Him to grow you in these areas.

FOR ALL YOU'RE WORTH

"So don't be afraid; you are worth more than many sparrows."   *Matthew 10:31*

For All You're Worth

Words by Bob Hartman
Music by Jim Cooper
© 1995 Petsong Pub. (admin. by Word, Inc.)/SESAC/Jimmy Vision Music/BMI. All rights reserved. International copyright secured. Used by permission.

Chorus
Hold on to life for all you're worth,
you know He died for all you're worth.
He loves you, you have the greatest
value. He gave His life for all,
for all you're worth.

By this time you know the story, there's
nothing there you haven't heard.
You can cross the line of knowing and
your heart believing His word.
Do you think He brought you this far
just to leave you wondering where and
who you are? Just think back to where it
began—Jesus called your name and
then you just took His hand.

Repeat chorus

Even gold still needs refining, burning
off impurities. Even diamonds grow in
value when they're cut so carefully.
There's no life beyond His repair,
you will find Him waiting just
beyond a prayer. He invested all
that He had, don't you think it
hurts Him inside to see you sad?

Repeat chorus

He has His eye on you, you have the
greatest value. He gave His life
for all, for all you're worth,
for all you're worth.

I believe one of the most dangerous trends in our culture is the devaluation of human life. With all the violence we see in the media, we can start to become numb to the value of life, and sometimes even the value of our own lives. All of us have felt totally worthless at times. "For All You're Worth" emphasizes the fact that we are each a unique and wonderful creation of God, endowed with dignity and worth from our Creator, and as Christians, we are temples for God's Holy Spirit.

In this Scripture from Matthew, Jesus compares our value to that of a sparrow. A sparrow was one of the lowliest creatures of that day. They were so common that two could be purchased for about $1 \frac{1}{2}$ cents. The message is very clear. If the Father cares so much for the lowly sparrow that He knows each time one falls to the ground, how much more does He care for you and me, who are worth the very life of His Son! We cannot even comprehend how much we are worth to God. It's ourselves that need convincing.

Psychologists talk about things like low self-esteem and a negative self-image. These conditions result when we don't see ourselves the way God sees us. He has a perfect plan for every one of us and He is preparing a place for us to dwell with Him throughout eternity. If that doesn't raise your spirits, I don't know what will!

Take time today to look in the mirror and tell yourself the truth. You are a child of God purchased by the very blood of Jesus! You are loved beyond measure by your heavenly Father who is watching over you every minute of every day.

WE HOLD OUR HEARTS OUT TO YOU

"Then make my joy complete by being like-minded, having the same love, being one in spirit and purpose."

Philippians 2:2

We Hold Our Hearts Out to You

Words by Bob Hartman
Music by John Elefante and Dino Elefante
© 1995 Petsong Pub. (admin. by Word, Inc.)/
SESAC/Uncle Pitts Music/BMI. All rights reserved.
International copyright secured. Used by permission.

Here we are gathered once again under
Your Name, thinking of the ways
we all have caused You shame.
But we can find consolation in the things
that You said. We are all bound in our
hearts by a common thread. We look to
You who made us one to give us
strength and bring our hearts
back to where we've begun.

Chorus
So, together we hold all our hearts out
to You, and we all can believe
You know just what to do.
Heal and forgive us, make us all
just like new, Jesus, we hold
our hearts out to You, Jesus,
we hold our hearts out to You.

Sometimes we forget what it is that
brings us here, sometimes we forget
what it means to be sincere.
And there are times we are bothered
when we don't seem to feel, then we all
focus on the One who makes things real.
We look around and we feel strong, we
feel Your presence then we know that
this is where we belong.

Repeat Chorus

And when we hold out all our lost and
shattered dreams, You will be binding
every heart with broken seams.
With a warm and loving hand,
You understand.

Repeat Chorus

I really had youth groups in mind when I wrote the lyrics for this song. There is a mysterious dynamic that takes place when two or more of us are gathered in His name. Jesus said, "'For where two or three come together in my name, there am I with them'" (Matthew 18:20). In much the same way that Jesus appeared to His disciples after His resurrection, He also "appears" to us by His Spirit when we are gathered in His name.

The first verse of this song talks about the feeling we get when we go to our church or fellowship right after we have really blown it. We look around and wonder if anybody knows. Then we feel like a hypocrite when we begin to participate. This is a very effective tactic of the enemy. Sometimes we don't even want to go because we feel so bad. But when we finally get there and begin to feel the presence of God, everything starts to make sense. We experience His forgiveness, mercy and healing. It is then that we remember why we are there.

We desperately need these times regularly. This is why Hebrews 10:25 tells us, "Let us not give up meeting together, as some are in the habit of doing, but let us encourage one another—and all the more as you see the Day approaching." The coming together of believers in His name is essential and beneficial to every believer. In fact, if you are not part of a regular fellowship, you are out of the will of God.

Why not make plans right now to attend the next meeting of your church or fellowship? I am confident you will find others just like you, holding out their hearts to God, saying, "Heal and forgive us, make us all just like new."

WE NEED JESUS

"On hearing this, Jesus said, 'It is not the healthy who need a doctor, but the sick.'"   *Matthew 9:12*

We Need Jesus

Words and music by John and Dino Elefante
and Scott Springer
© 1997 by Uncle Pitts Music/Dayspring Music/BMI.
All rights reserved. International copyright secured.
Used by permission.

Chorus
When will the world see
that we need Jesus?
If we open our eyes we will
all realize that He loves us.
When will the world see
that we need Jesus?
When our hearts are as one and
believe that He's the Son of our God.

The Lord is our God and we shall
never want. The Lord is our God
and we shall live forever.
When we share the love of Jesus,
see each other as he sees us
then His love will see us through,
His love will see us through.

When will the world see
that we need Jesus?
When sister and brother
love one another as one.
When will the world see
that we need Jesus?
Will we ever understand
Jesus is the Son of man?
We must live in the
shadow of His love.

Repeat chorus

This world is sick but Jesus heals! This song was previously recorded by John and Dino Elefante on their label (Pakaderm) on the *Portrait of a Spirit* project. When considering songs for Petra's newest praise recording, I wanted very much to record this tune. When it came time to decide on a title, I realized how fitting it was that we subtitle the album *We Need Jesus*. It is the cry and desire of each one of our hearts as Christians that the world see that we all need Jesus. Unless we recognize our sickness, how can we seek a cure?

The song answers this rhetorical question with several answers that all point back to us! The world will see when *we* open *our* eyes and realize that He loves us, when our hearts are as one, when we believe He's the Son of God. Only when we believe that He loves us in spite of our sinfulness and selfishness can we feel compelled to share that love with a world which is searching for true love yet sometimes believes that such a love does not exist.

Matthew 9:12 is Jesus' reply to the question of why He spent time with the biggest sinners of that day. They knew they were sick, but the Son of God spent time with them. Perhaps for the first time in their lives they felt loved. Many of them became some of Jesus' most loyal followers. Jesus' love took Him all the way to the cross, for "while we were still sinners, Christ died for us" (Romans 5:8). There is hope for this world in Jesus, for if He loved and transformed you and me, He will do the same for others when we "live in the shadow of His love."

God wants us to show the world what true love is, and we must allow that love to permeate every part of our lives.

It's been ten years since Bob Hartman first called me. Since that time, God has had a tremendous call on my and my brother's life to make Christian records—and one thing remains constant in every decision. We find ourselves asking, "What would Bob do?" How would he deal with this situation—through God's eyes, in prayer? How would he respond in compassion, fairness and wisdom?

I am a die-hard Petra fan and am honored to be a part of their ministry. Much has come from my association with Petra. Picture this . . . John and I sitting at the studio board while Lou Gramm (singer for Foreigner, now a two-year-old believer) is singing our song, "We Need Jesus." Bob Hartman and John Schlitt are sitting behind us, smiling from ear to ear. The song's kickin', the track's kickin', Lou's kickin' . . . who needs respect?

—Dino Elefante

BE OF GOOD CHEER

" I have told you these things, so that in me you may have peace. In this world you will have trouble. But take heart! I have overcome the world.'" John 16:33

Be of Good Cheer
Words & music by Bob Hartman
© 1997 Petsong Pub. (admin. by Word,
Inc.)/SESAC. All rights reserved. International
copyright secured. Used by permission.

Peace be unto you,
my peace I give to you.
In this world you'll surely find trials
of many different kinds, but . . .

Chorus
Be of good cheer, be of good cheer,
for I have overcome this world.
Be of good cheer, be of good cheer.

For now I go away but I will return
to take you to a place to dwell
so where I am you'll be as well.

Repeat chorus

In this world you'll surely find
trials of many different kinds,
but I will not forsake you,
then I'll be with you until the end.

Repeat chorus

In this song from Petra's second praise album, I put one of my favorite Scriptures to music. I have always found great comfort in this statement of contrast from our Lord. In the previous verse, we find the "things" Jesus told His disciples, things that caused them to doubt and fear. They would desert Jesus after He was arrested. But even in this solemn prophecy of their failure, He told them that even though they would forsake Him, He would never be alone, for His Father is forever with Him.

We also are encouraged that we can have peace in Jesus, even though we will have many tribulations and persecutions. We can "be of good cheer." This is not some false sense of security, but a true peace that "transcends our understanding," a peace that comes from faith in the One who has "overcome the world." If we grasp what Jesus said in this verse, our way of looking at this world will be radically transformed.

There is a prevalent attitude in modern Christianity that God's job is to smooth out all the rough spots in our lives. This belief leads to great disheartening when trials *do* come to us. We wonder why God didn't spare us from our misery and blame ourselves for lack of faith or some sin that caused God to "forsake" us. Jesus tells us that we *will* have trouble in this world. Yet through the worst storms, we can still have peace in Him, knowing that He is our victory.

He has overcome this world and we can as well, "for everyone born of God overcomes the world. This is the victory that has overcome the world, even our faith. Who is it that overcomes the world? Only he who believes that Jesus is the Son of God" (1 John 5:4, 5).

We recently completed our eighth record with Bob and a slightly different Petra, but it felt the same. When Bob's song, "Lovely Lord," or Jim Cooper's "Song of Moses" hits my ears, it takes me back . . . back to when I first saw what made them cooler than us. It was the fact that the devil hated what they were doing with such a passion that he inflicted death and devastation upon us and our families every time we would start a Petra record. Louie's 16-year-old nephew, Petra's sound man, Michael T., my aunt and niece were all taken during the recording of Petra's albums.

Many things have happened in the course of our history with Petra: member changes, Gold records, Grammys, Dove awards, respect and applause from the industry. Through the high points and low points (being "fired" for one record), we never ceased to love, admire and respect the guys in Petra.
—Dino Elefante

SCRIPTURE INDEX

SONG INDEX